Passport to Success

OTHER TITLES OF INTEREST BY
ROWMAN & LITTLEFIELD EDUCATION

Working for Kids: Educational Leadership as Inquiry and Invention
By James H. Lytle

The Principal as School Manager, Third Edition
By William L. Sharp and James K. Walter

*School District Master Planning:
A Practical Guide to Demographics and Facilities Planning*
By Kelley D. Carey

Engaging Students: Using the Unit in Comprehensive Lesson Planning
By Dianna P. Beirne and Kathleen G. Velsor

*Achieving Success for Kids:
A Plan for Returning to Core Values, Beliefs, and Principles*
By Tim L. Adsit

Going Back to the Future: A Leadership Journey for Educators
By Robert Palestini

Leading for Democracy: A Case-Based Approach to Principal Preparation
By Patrick M. Jenlink, Lee Stewart, and Sandra Stewart

Passport to Success

Strategic Planning at the Personal and Professional Levels

Tim L. Adsit

ROWMAN & LITTLEFIELD EDUCATION

A division of
ROWMAN & LITTLEFIELD PUBLISHERS, INC.
Lanham • New York • Toronto • Plymouth, UK

Published by Rowman & Littlefield Education
A division of Rowman & Littlefield Publishers, Inc.
A wholly owned subsidiary of The Rowman & Littlefield Publishing Group, Inc.
4501 Forbes Boulevard, Suite 200, Lanham, Maryland 20706
www.rowman.com

10 Thornbury Road, Plymouth PL6 7PP, United Kingdom

Copyright © 2013 by Tim L. Adsit

All rights reserved. No part of this book may be reproduced in any form or by any electronic or mechanical means, including information storage and retrieval systems, without written permission from the publisher, except by a reviewer who may quote passages in a review.

British Library Cataloguing in Publication Information Available

Library of Congress Cataloging-in-Publication Data

Adsit, Tim L., 1948-
  Passport to success : strategic planning at the personal and professional levels / Tim L. Adsit.
       p. cm.
  Includes bibliographical references.
  ISBN 978-1-61048-525-8 (pbk.)—ISBN 978-1-61048-526-5 (electronic)
  1. Educational planning—United States. 2. Strategic planning—Education—United States. 3. School management and organization—United States. I. Title.
  LC89.A125 2013
  371.200973—dc23
                                                                            2012031163

DEDICATION

If you don't know where you are going, you are certain to end up somewhere else.

—Yogi Berra

I dedicate this book to my colleagues and clients in public and private schools who have implemented successful strategic plans, my mentors, my close personal friends, and my children, grandchildren, parents, and family.

EPIGRAPH

You were born to win, but to be a winner, you must plan to win, prepare to win, and expect to win.

—Zig Ziglar

YOUR PASSPORT TO SUCCESS: STRATEGIC PLANNING AT THE PERSONAL AND PROFESSIONAL LEVELS

Passports are resources you use to get from one destination to another. They typically contain the information required to pass through "checkpoints" and meet the standards of your desired location and goals you are seeking to achieve. You can also use the "passport" analogy to describe tools that help us gain personal and professional success, such as:

- Strategic planning
- Career growth
- Personal life planning
- Business development
- Financial planning

CREATE YOUR FUTURE USING THIS PRACTICAL GUIDE

Whether you work in a small, medium, or large school organization; are independent or self-employed; work in a large corporation or organization; or are part of a professional service firm or team, this book will guide you to look ahead and plan a successful professional future and satisfying personal life. This book will help you:

- Clarify your personal, career, and financial objectives
- Determine appropriate career alternatives and changes
- Prepare a personal and professional mission statement and strategic plan
- Identify your own "driving force," the one strategic core value that will be your ultimate decision-making factor
- Establish long-term objectives to position where you want to be at specific points in the future
- Develop a strategic action plan designed to accomplish your long-term objectives

SYSTEMATIC WAY OF THINKING

Brian Tracy tells us,

Skill in personal strategic planning is not something you are born with, like eye color or perfect pitch. It is a systematic way of thinking and acting and is, therefore, something you can learn, like riding a bike or changing a tire. With practice, you can master the many different elements that make up this key skill, and you will get into the rhythm of thinking and acting strategically for the rest of your life. When you do acquire rhythm, you will realize extraordinary results. Your life and career will take off, and the sky is truly the limit.

Save Time and Money

Why is strategic planning and thinking so helpful? The answer is simple: it saves you an enormous amount of time and money. When you review and analyze key strategic questions of concepts of your career or business, you find yourself focusing on the critical tasks necessary to achieve your goals. At the same time, you stop doing those things that keep you from achieving success. You do more of the right things and fewer things that get and keep you off track. You set performance goals for people and projects. You become skilled at measuring and tracking results. You move into the express lane in both work and life. (Brian Tracy, March 7, 2011)

Contents

Foreword	xi
Preface	xiii
Acknowledgments	xvii
1 Introduction and Overview	1
2 A Brief Review of the Literature on Strategic Planning Including Organizational/Institutional, Departmental, Educational, and Personal	7
3 Strategic Planning for Extraordinary Change in the New Information Age, Global Economy of the Twenty-First Century	17
4 Brief Case Study Examples of Effective Strategic Plans in the Field of Education	23
5 The Process and Tools for Organizational and Departmental Strategic Planning in Education	35
6 The Process and Tools for Personal Strategic Planning	39
7 Personal Strategic Plan Summary	65
References	71
About the Author	75

Foreword

> The result of planning should be effective, efficient, and economical. . . . that is, suitable for the intended purpose, capable of producing the desired results, and involving the least investment of resources.
>
> —Clark Crouch

Passport to Success is focused upon several important elements in the area of long-term planning—the history of the strategic planning movement, the value of applying effective strategic planning techniques in forming a personal plan, the experience of school districts in using strategic planning, and tools for developing a personal strategic plan.

The first portion of the book serves an important purpose in drawing together references and excerpts of writing on the topic of strategic planning in general. The literature surrounding strategic planning is spotty in terms of identifying the degree of success that practitioners have achieved and the particular approaches most likely to be successful. A picture emerges that is helpful in identifying the steps that have most usually characterized the work.

The concept of applying strategic planning to the life of an individual, in the direction taken by author Dr. Tim Adsit, is somewhat unusual. The challenge of organizing one's life in a strategic manner is in a general sense the subject of countless books, programs, courses, and self-help efforts. Dr. Adsit approaches this with a different mindset, extracting the steps of sound strategic planning and then combining them with a broad array of personal values including the spiritual. This provides a contribution to the literature that seems unusual and provocative.

The discussion of strategic planning efforts in the field of education highlights the general experience of educational systems across the country and over several decades. One of the real values of this section of the book is that it points out that the process of strategic planning may be the most valuable result of the efforts invested. Very little research seems evident as to whether the hoped-for goals of improving educational achievement have been directly produced by strategic planning work. That is not to say they have not, but simply to say that the balance of written evidence does not support that conclusion. School districts have to plan in some fashion, and using a strategic planning approach offers a structure in which to do so.

Dr. Adsit has reported some of the pitfalls for school districts to avoid and some of the factors that should be built into the effort—this is a helpful service for school districts. Perhaps the most important point, in this writer's opinion, is the book's emphasis on being responsive to change, the value of garnering support from stakeholders, and the ability to adapt as needed.

Dr. Adsit also provides information on how to use a strategic planning approach to help meet one's personal goals, He touches upon a wide array of considerations with reference to people who have written about particular approaches. He also describes a "how-to" structure with planning diagrams and forms—in combination, he offers a workbook approach to this dimension.

A final word on the book: drawing together the wide spectrum of references on the subject of strategic planning is a valuable service in itself. Were one to undertake a search of the literature on strategic planning, it would be very difficult to find all of the resources that Tim Adsit has collected. It is worthwhile to review this book to gain perspective and to consider how strategic planning can be beneficial organizationally and on a personal level.

Michael R. Boring, EdD
October 2011

Dr. Michael R. Boring, EdD, has been involved with educational administration for over thirty years and currently has a consulting practice with school districts across the state of Washington.

Preface

> Personal strategic planning is a disciplined thought process, which produces fundamental decisions and actions that shape and guide who you are, where you are going, what you do, and how, when and why you do it. All of this is done with a focus on the future.
>
> —Gary Ryan Blair

Passport to Success is about personal strategic planning. The primary purpose of personal strategic planning is to find balance between your career and your life and to plan for continuous improvement in all thirteen major areas of your life. These thirteen major areas of your life include: spiritual, family, physical, mental, social/emotional, career/vocational/professional, educational/intellectual, recreational, financial, health, housing, transportation, and parenting goals. The basic planning process involves assessment (where you are), setting goals and objectives (where you want to be), and creating an action plan (how to get there). Think of it as a road map and passport to your future and success.

WHY A PERSONAL STRATEGIC PLAN?

A personal strategic plan is one way a person can take control of his or her life and career. By assessing your status in the thirteen areas of your life and deciding where you would like to be, you can take the necessary steps to reach your personal goals. As Gary Ryan Blair states, "The purpose of personal strategic planning is to help you:

- Provide direction, meaning, and purpose for your life;
- Make decisions that positively affect your future;

- Focus your energies on what's most important;
- Achieve the greatest results in the shortest period of time;
- Significantly increase your level of performance;
- Enjoy more time, money, balance, and freedom;
- Eliminate uncertainty, anxiety, doubt, and fear;
- Leverage your skills more effectively;
- Enhance your quality of life and overall peace of mind; and
- Be more, do more, and ultimately to have more from life." (Gary Ryan Blair, Create a Personal Strategic Plan!, www.motivationalcentral.com/goal-setitngs-personal-strategic-plan.html, p.1)

This book really started around 2009 in a phone conversation between Tim L. Adsit and Thomas F. Koerner, PhD (vice president and editorial director, Rowman & Littlefield Education), in which they discussed the concept of personal strategic planning and Dr. Koerner's level of interest in reviewing a formal proposal for a book on the subject.

Tim explained that, while there are several good books on the market dealing with corporate, small business, nonprofit, organizational, and departmental strategic planning, what makes this book unique is that it also adds the third dimension and component of "personal strategic planning," which, after all, is of most importance to individuals. Dr. Koerner encouraged Tim to submit a proposal in the future when the timing was right. The author brings many years of successful experience in strategic planning in school districts and in facilitating the development and implementation of successful personal strategic plans.

This book is primarily about personal strategic planning, which is defined by several authors as:

> A disciplined thought process, which produces fundamental decisions and actions that shape and guide who you are, where you are going, what you do, and how, when and why you do it. All of this is done with a focus on the future. (Gary Ryan Blair, Create a Personal Strategic Plan!, p.1)

> A program to think, plan, and act strategically at all personal levels. (Adapted from www.CMOE.com/strategic-thinking.htm)

And finally, the author's definition of personal strategic planning is a systematic program and cyclic process designed to manage one's future by thinking; by identifying a personal mission, vision, set of core beliefs and values, core competencies, life skills, and lifelong guidelines; and by identifying strategic challenges and advantages, contingency plans, objectives, goals, hopes, dreams, aspirations, performance indicators for measuring success and achievement, strategies, tactics, action plans, alignment, and balance in all areas of one's life. These areas include spiritual, family, physical, mental, social/emotional, career/vocational/professional, educational/intellectual, recreational, financial, health, housing, transportation, and parenting goals. In this process, one can become truly successful, achieve life's goals, leave a significant legacy, and achieve self-actualization and personal satisfaction.

The book is organized into the following chapters:

- Chapter 1—Introduction and Overview
- Chapter 2—A Brief Review of the Literature on Strategic Planning Including Organizational/Institutional, Departmental, Educational, and Personal
- Chapter 3—Strategic Planning for Extraordinary Change in the New Information Age, Global Economy of the Twenty-First Century
- Chapter 4—Brief Case Study Examples of Effective Strategic Plans from the Field of Education
- Chapter 5—The Process and Tools for Organizational and Departmental Strategic Planning in Education
- Chapter 6—The Process and Tools for Personal Strategic Planning
- Chapter 7—Personal Strategic Plan Summary

The author has designed this book as a "how-to" tool for strategic planning in education at all levels, including organization, departmental, and individual. This book provides step-by-step strategies and practices for developing an institutional strategic plan, implementing the effort through departmental planning, and realizing the goals of the plan through the development of teams and personal/professional planning. Through theory, practice, working tools, and the other training materials needed to create, implement, and realize strategic plans, *Passport to Success: Strategic Planning at the Personal and Professional Levels* will simplify your work of educational strategic planning, whether as an everyday practitioner, manager, or leader, and give you a template and process to follow to develop your own personal strategic life plan that is linked to your organization's strategic plan.

POINTS TO REMEMBER

- The primary purpose of personal strategic planning is to find balance between your career and your life and to plan for continuous improvement in all thirteen major areas of your life. These thirteen major areas of your

life include: Spiritual, family, physical, mental, social/emotional, career/vocational/professional, educational/intellectual, recreational, financial, health, housing, transportation, and parenting goals.
- The basic planning process involves assessment (where you are), setting goals and objectives (where you want to be), and creating an action plan (how to get there). Think of it as a road map and passport to your future and success.
- "The purpose of personal strategic planning is to help you:

  - Provide direction, meaning, and purpose for your life;
  - Make decisions that positively affect your future;
  - Focus your energies on what's most important;
  - Achieve the greatest results in the shortest period of time;
  - Significantly increase your level of performance;
  - Enjoy more time, money, balance, and freedom;
  - Eliminate uncertainty, anxiety, doubt, and fear;
  - Leverage your skills more effectively;
  - Enhance your quality of life and overall peace of mind; and
  - Be more, do more, and ultimately to have more from life." (Gary Ryan Blair, Create a Personal Strategic Plan!, www.motivationalcentral.com/goal-setitngs-personal-strategic-plan.html, p.1)

- Personal strategic planning is the process of determining a person's short and long-term goals and then identifying the best approach for achieving those goals.
- Personal strategic planning is a process by which an individual envisions his/her future and develops the necessary procedures and operations to achieve that future.

Acknowledgments

You see things and say "Why?" But I dream things that never were; and I say "Why not?"

—George Bernard Shaw

The author would like to acknowledge the following mentors, colleagues, and authors who have profoundly affected his thinking about strategic planning in one way or another, and who have contributed greatly to his professional career, growth, and personal success in life to date: Reverend Glyn B. Adsit; Dr. William J. Austin; Jerry Bennett; Glenn Bland; Gary Ryan Blair; Dr. Michael R. Boring; Dr. Bill Cook; Dr. Kate Dickson; Jeannie Magmer; Dr. George L. Morrisey; Dr. Jerry Patterson; Dr. Philip Piele; and Dr. Jim Ulum.

Chapter One

Introduction and Overview

Leaders establish the vision for the future and set the strategy for getting there; they cause change. They motivate and inspire others to go in the right direction and they, along with everyone else, sacrifice to get there.

—John Kotter

We will either find a way, or make one.

—Hannibal

This author is convinced from all his research and practical experience—as a successful coach, teacher, principal, director of curriculum, grant writer, organizational change agent, superintendent, management consultant, independent business owner, and author with experience in instruction, assessment, human resources, rural schools, and school improvement—that we are in the midst of an era of great change, challenge, and opportunity for educational organizations and the individuals who comprise them.

Current leadership and management writings suggest that educational organizations resistant to changing their management theory are predetermined toward failure. Simultaneously, those educational organizations that adopt new paradigms and new mental models while neglecting to transform their daily business practices such as strategic planning are merely putting lipstick on the pig to dress it up. It is the individuals working within the school organizations who need to transform practice, the conceptualization of work, and their ideals to match the new leadership paradigms.

School organizations should realize and confront the new realities that confront them. They should develop a strategic planning process that is designed to promote change and sensible, reasonable risk-taking. The process should address the competitive demands of the post-industrial, twenty-first-century, information-age world of ever-increasing knowledge, technology, and global complexity.

All public and private schools in America must strive to meet or exceed both national and international world-class standards for education to be competitive in a global economy. This author has laid out a strategic action plan for reaching national standards in two years and international standards two years after that. The reader is encouraged to read a new book entitled *Achieving Success for Kids: A Plan for Returning to Core Values, Beliefs, and Principles* (Rowman & Littlefield Education, Lanham, MD, 2011), and to implement the strategic plans outlined therein.

Our process of strategic planning in school organizations should address the emergent environments, cultures, and structures that challenge school leaders. The process should focus on the current construction of the school organization, addressing both short- and long-term effectiveness; and, finally, it should embrace chaos in an attempt to create order. We must thrive on chaos, harness it, and make it work favorably for our school organizations.

A new strategic planning process, which Dr. William J. Austin calls "triadic heterarchial strategic planning," suggests that all (school) executives and staff be given greater decision-making power and a larger sphere of influence throughout the planning process. Austin's new process "further demonstrates that power and influence are guided by principles of trust and responsibility when the emphasis is on collaboration and win-win outcomes." His model shows "that an emphasis on quality is paramount in the development of an organizational-planning-and-outcomes model where measurements of success emphasize institutional, departmental, and personal outcomes over the planning process. . . ." Finally, his book entitled *Strategic Planning for Smart Leadership* "demonstrates that organizational traditions and standards should come into question and should be reviewed systematically" (William J. Austin, 2002, p. 4).

Austin's process is dramatically different from traditional models of strategic planning that emphasize the conventional hierarchy, command-and-control, and development of plans through a standard systemic process. In this sort of traditional planning, brainstorming is key and the central decision for leaders is whether the plan should occur every year, every three years, or every five years.

In the traditional strategic planning practices, there is a disparity between the individuals' values and the organization's values. Even where there is a goal for the establishment of a common vision, mission, and values, there is not a process in which employees are encouraged to internalize the vision, mission, and values.

The nature of the problem, as Austin describes it,

> is the gap between individual responsibility and departmental/institutional responsibility. . . .The current issue with the traditional planning process is that it fails to address (a) opening honest, prudent lines of cross-institutional communication, (b) building trust throughout the (school) organization, (c) creating a system of motivation, (d) ensuring professional treatment of all employees, and (e) the creating of a system that integrates the values of all employees with the mission and plans of the (district, its departments, the school(s), and the individuals that work within them). (As adapted from Austin, pp. 4–5.)

One central goal of this book is to stress personalized strategic planning and describe a comprehensive planning process that unites the individual planning projects of the school district. Planning at the level of the district is then integrated with planning at the level of the department. Planning at the department level is integrated with planning at the self-directed work team and/or individual level. The entire process is solidified through the integration of both the budgeting process and the human resource appraisal (evaluation) system.

Basically, Austin's book has already described this process in great detail, using diagrams and written workbook pages, and you are referred to his work, *Strategic Planning for Smart Leadership*, to get a greater understanding of how the process works.

However, in this author's opinion, Austin's book makes its greatest contribution to emergent models of strategic planning in education in its detailed description of and emphasis on individual or personalized strategic planning and demonstration of how it links to district, departmental, and team strategic planning.

Once the three-level (triadic) process is in place, the emphasis on the top of the hierarchy, the traditional model, is diminished by turning the entire process upside-down (i.e., the personal planning process suggests the need for departmental planning, which then identifies institutional needs and strategies). When this strategy is initiated, managing the organization evolves from a hierarchical model to an emergent heterarchy, as Austin calls it (as adapted from Austin, p. 6).

This book is basically designed as a practitioner's "how-to" book for strategic planning at all levels of the school district organization. Among the benefits of the book is its step-by-step strategies and practices that enable the reader to develop an institutional strategic plan, implement the plan through departmental planning, and realize the goals of the plan through the development of high-performance teams and individual-personal-professional planning.

The main issue for the successful school district organization of the twenty-first century is how to efficiently structure this complex organization to improve effectiveness, productivity, and innovation. The main mission of all schools, in this author's opinion, is to continuously improve student learning and achievement.

Just as continuously increasing levels of differentiation limit our current understanding of organizational structure, trying to manage hierarchial structures in an era of ultra-differentiation continues to prove increasingly unproductive. The best and brightest leadership scholars have come to a common consensus that structuring our (school) organizations within a hierarchy leads to failure (Belasco, 1999; Bolman and Deal, 1997; Bridges, 1996; Handy, 1996; Helgesen, 1996; Knoke, 1996; Lawler, 1996; Lucas, 1997; Pinchot, 1994; Schein, 1992; Senge, 1996; and Wheatley, 1996).

POINTS TO REMEMBER

- We are in the midst of an era of great change, challenge, and opportunity for educational organizations and the individuals who comprise them.
- All public and private schools in America must strive to meet or exceed both national and international world-class standards for education to be competitive in a global economy. This author has laid out a strategic action plan for reaching national standards in two years and international standards in two more years after that. If you have not already done so, you are encouraged to read a new book entitled *Achieving Success for Kids: A Plan for Returning to Core Values, Beliefs, and Principles* (Rowman and Littlefield Education, Lanham, MD, 2011), and to implement the strategic plans outlined therein.
- A new strategic planning process, which Dr. William J. Austin calls "triadic heterarchial strategic planning," suggests that all (school) executives and staff should be given greater decision-making power and a larger sphere of influence throughout the planning process.
- One central goal of this book is to stress personalized strategic planning and describe a comprehensive planning process that unites the individual planning projects of the school district. Planning at the level of the district is then integrated with planning at the level of the department. Planning at the department level is integrated with planning at the self-directed work team and/or individual level. The entire process is solidified through the integration of both the budgeting process and the human resource appraisal (evaluation) system.

- This book is designed to be a practitioner's "how-to" book for strategic planning at all levels of the school district organization. The book will provide step-by-step strategies and practices to develop an institutional strategic plan, implement the plan through departmental planning, and realize the goals of the plan through the development of high-performance teams and individual-personal-professional planning.

Chapter Two

A Brief Review of the Literature on Strategic Planning Including Organizational/Institutional, Departmental, Educational, and Personal

Vision without action is a dream. Action without vision is simply passing the time. Action with vision is making a positive difference and can change the world.

—Joel Barker

BRIEF HISTORY OF STRATEGIC PLANNING

Military Roots

The history of strategic planning begins in the military. According to Webster's *New World Dictionary*, strategy is "the science of planning and directing large-scale military operations, of maneuvering forces into the most advantageous position prior to actual engagement with the enemy" (Guralnik, 1986).

Although our understanding of strategy as applied in management has been transformed, one element remains key: aim to achieve competitive advantage. Taking its name and roots from the military model, early models of formal strategic planning "reflected the hierarchical values and linear systems of traditional organizations. Undertaken by elite planning functions at the top of the organization, its structure was highly vertical and time-bound. A certain period would be set aside to analyze the situation and decide on a course of action. This would result in a formal document. Once this was done, the actual work of implementation—which was considered a separate, discrete process—could begin" (Wall and Wall, 1995).

Although individual definitions of strategy vary between authors, traditionally, theorists have considered planning an essential part of organizational strategy.

Business

Strategic planning in business organizations originated in the 1950s and was very popular and widespread between mid-1960s to mid-1970s, when people believed it was the answer for all problems, and corporate America was "obsessed" with strategic planning. Following that "boom," strategic planning was cast aside and abandoned for over a decade. The 1990s brought the revival of strategic planning as a "process with particular benefits in particular contexts" (Mintzberg, 1994).

Here is a brief account of several generations of strategic planning. The *SWOT* analysis model dominated strategic planning of the 1950s. "The 1960s brought qualitative and quantitative models of strategy. During the early 1980s, the shareholder value model and the *Porter model* became the standard. The rest of the 1980s was dictated by strategic intent and core competencies, and market-focused organizations. Finally, business transformation became de rigueur in the 1990s" (Gouillart, 1995).

Subsequent newer models of strategic planning were focused on adaptability to change, flexibility, and importance of strategic thinking and organizational learning. "Strategic agility" is becoming more important than the strategy itself, because the organization's ability to succeed "has more to do with its ability to transform itself, continuously, than whether it has the right strategy. Being strategically agile enables organizations to transform their strategy depending on the changes in their environment" (Gouillart, 1995).

Only recently have newer business models of strategic planning realized the need to include personalized strategic planning. For example, Mazur (2007) states,

> A personal strategic plan can help any professional or business owner (we are all self-employed as personal career managers responsible for our own success) to gain power and take control. A plan can make the difference between being trapped and being empowered. . . . Having strategy and focus in your business life, and a mess in your personal life is likely to prevent you from achieving personal success, even if you achieve astounding business success.
>
> Research shows that if an individual sets only career-related goals, they usually fail to achieved them or remain unsatisfied upon their achievement. When an individual sets goals that take their whole life into account, they are more likely to succeed and realize satisfaction that will inspire them on to even greater accomplishment. . . . Planning for personal success should be approached with just as much diligence as planning for a successful business. (Mazur, 2007, pp. 1–2)

Likewise, Dr. Dahl (2008) introduced a book entitled *Optimize Your Life! 2008 Workbook Edition*, which presents a new approach to strategic thinking and planning called STP. As early as 1981, Dr. Dahl recognized that the strategic plan of an organization was nothing more than the merging of the personal strategic plans of the key people of the organization. Organizations do not have values, missions, visions, or goals, but the key people in the organization have them at the personal level.

His model following classic organizational strategic planning, developed over more than twenty-five years of successful experience, has been very successfully modified and adapted for personal use. The model has worked well for individual strategic planning, small business, large corporations, nonprofit entities, and school organizations.

Another pioneer in the next generation of strategic planning in business, health care, higher education, and education is William Austin (2002). Dr. Austin wrote a book entitled *Strategic Planning for Smart Leadership*. This book is a first-rate nuts-and-bolts how-to guide to the next generation of strategic planning, and his workbook approach is commendable and useful. His book

> reviews relevant planning, management, and leadership literature to create the context for a heterarchical (as opposed to hierarchial) planning system within the theoretical framework of contemporary leadership, planning, human resource development, and systems thinking. It is designed to provide institutions that enter the planning process with no idea of where it might take them with achievable ideals of where their planning process should lead them.
>
> The author designed this book as a "how-to" tool for strategic planning at all levels of the organization. This proven book provides step-by-step strategies and practices for developing an institutional strategic plan, implementing the effort through departmental planning, and realizing the goals of the plan through the development of teams and personal/professional planning. Through theory, practice, workbooks, and the other training materials needed to create, implement, and realize strategic plans, *Strategic Planning for Smart Leadership* will simplify the work of strategic planning for the everyday practitioner, manager, or leader. (Austin, 2002)

In conducting a literature review in preparation for this book, the author found that strategic planning books abound. Some are academically oriented; others are more practical and immediately useful. Some are not very substantive, while others are deep and cause the reader to reflect. You may wish to look at a few of the following books to determine which might best guide your own planning efforts:

1. Bryan W. Barry, *Strategic Planning Workbook for Nonprofit Organizations*, Amherst H. Wilder Foundation, St. Paul (1986).

   How do you reach your goals and make an impact when you're faced with funding cuts and increased competition? You'll find the answer in this practical guide, a straightforward primer with worksheets. It discusses time and/or budget constraints, and how to overcome obstacles to create a winning strategic plan. Step-by-step instructions help you develop sound, realistic plans for the future. You'll learn how to:

- Solve a web of problems that are hard to address one by one
- Build teamwork, improve communication, and boost managerial skills
- Influence rather than be influenced—especially in this time of new federal cutbacks
- Survive, even thrive, with fewer resources
- Stimulate forward thinking and refocus your mission

Written by national strategic planning expert Bryan Barry, this updated edition builds on the original and adds new sections so that you get:

- Step-by-step guidance through the five planning steps
- Four methods for developing a plan
- Critical ingredients of a sound plan
- Information on how to create a shared vision of your nonprofit's future to guide staff in making everyday choices
- Strategies to address problems and opportunities that the nonprofit sector now faces
- A new, more detailed sample of one nonprofit's actual three-year plan, including goals, strategies, staffing, financial, and implementation plans
- New suggestions on how to format your plan
- Additional tips for implementing and updating your plan
- A sample three-year plan
- Examples of how multiple organizations, coalitions, and communities can use strategic planning
- A CD-ROM with easy-to-complete, interactive worksheets to help you develop your own plan, sell it to your colleagues, and measure results
- Completed worksheet samples

With the *Strategic Planning Workbook* you'll get a clear sense of direction that will guide your choices about which opportunities to pursue and which to avoid!
2. Patrick J. Below, George L. Morrisey, and Betty L. Acomb, *The Executive Guide to Strategic Planning*, Jossey-Bass, San Francisco (1990).

This book is a short, action-oriented guide, and one of the best on the market, in the author's opinion. It offers a comprehensive approach to strategic planning: how to formulate strategic plans that will develop the company's strengths, be responsive to changing business conditions, and chart a productive and profitable company future. The book provides numerous charts, worksheets, and other resources.

3. William S. Birnbaum, *If Your Strategy Is So Terrific, How Come It Doesn't Work?* American Management Association, New York (1990).

    The book offers clear guiding principles to making your strategic plan work.

4. Leonard Goodstein, Timothy Nolan, and J. William Pfeiffer, *Applied Strategic Planning: How to Develop a Plan Than Really Work*s, McGraw-Hill (1993).

    This book is a comprehensive guide to strategic planning. Written by three top consultants and trainers, *Applied Strategic Planning* shows managers and CEOs a clear, totally effective way to identify and implement strategic objectives.

    Applied Strategic Planning surpasses other strategic planning models in many key areas, including:

    - Emphasis on organizational culture
    - Integration of business and functional plans
    - Performance audits
    - Gap analysis
    - Values clarification

    Goodstein, Nolan, and Pfeiffer take managers through all phases of the strategic planning process, including how to:

    - Determine if an organization is ready for strategic planning
    - Effectively communicate a corporate vision
    - Recognize the role of culture in changing strategic direction
    - Understand the various roles of a consultant
    - Write effective mission statements
    - Create contingency plans containing charts, diagrams, and checklists, along with illuminating examples from the authors, extensive consulting experience, and even cartoons that convey important points. *Applied Strategic Planning* lets managers at the helm navigate expertly through today's unpredictable business climate.

5. Gary Hamel and C. K. Prahalad, *Competing for the Future*, Harvard Business School Press, Boston (1994).

    This is a classic book by two of the world's leading strategy consultants. Definitely business-oriented, the authors stress that winning in business today is not about being number one—it's about who "gets to the future first." In *Competing for the Future*, the authors urge companies to create their own futures, envision new markets, and reinvent themselves. And many of these same ideas apply to education.

6. George L. Morrisey, *Creating Your Future: Personal Strategic Planning for Professionals*, Berrett-Koehler, San Francisco (1992).

The book is aimed at individuals, but couples your plans with the organization's. It has a wonderful annotated bibliography. It's a great book on linking business strategic planning to personal strategic planning. Any professional, or aspiring professional, needs this book. A no-nonsense approach to a strategic career life plan, this book describes a complete step-by-step program for personal and professional success from one of our nation's foremost strategic planning experts. It's a practical guide to help professionals (within organizations and/or independent contractors) to use strategic planning for their own professional success and satisfying personal life. Worksheets, checklists, and charts help clarify personal values, financial concerns, career growth objectives, and business interests.

As Brian Tracy, author of *The Psychology of Success*, says, *Creating Your Future: Personal Strategic Planning for Professionals* is "perhaps the most important book on personal and professional goal setting and goal achieving ever put into print. Anyone who follows the simple, practical, step-by-step plan laid out in these pages will save themselves years of hard work."

7. George A. Steiner, *Strategic Planning: What Every Manager Must Know*, Free Press, New York (1979).

This is one of the seminal, classic texts in the field of strategic planning. Steiner's writing is always at the cutting edge of advanced thinking—yet firmly based on the solid ground of practical experience. Anyone who wants to keep his or her company in the front ranks of competition in a constantly changing world would be wise to read this book and to follow its clearly stated guidelines. Steiner takes planning out of the realm of high-flown abstractions and makes it a working tool that anyone can—and should—use in business or personal life.

In today's complex world of business, strategic planning is indispensable to effective management. Ever since the mid-1950s, when American companies began to develop formal long-range planning systems, wise managers have understood the importance of knowing where their firm was headed and how it intended to get there. To function effectively in a modern, planned operation, every manager must have a practical understanding of how the planning process works.

That's exactly what this book offers: a step-by-step guide to strategic planning. George A. Steiner, a well-known expert in the field of management, provides a concise, jargon-free handbook that avoids abstract theory and takes you straight to the "how-to" of planning. Whether you're designing and implementing a new plan or working with a plan that's already in operation, *Strategic Planning* puts the information you need at your fingertips. It takes you through every stage of the process, from idea to execution to evaluation (and explains "Fifty Common Pitfalls" you'll need to know about). You can plug your own data into the lucid charts, tables, and checklists for a valuable start on getting organized and evaluating your planning needs. And there's plenty of penetrating discussion about the questions and quandaries you're likely to meet along the way. For example:

- How do you identify, evaluate, and implement strategies?
- How do you design a planning system to fit the unique characteristics of you and your company?
- Can an intuitive manager do formal strategic planning?
- What are some ways to develop clear objectives?
- What human behavior factors can endanger planning and how can managers overcome them?
- How, and when, should a situation audit be made?
- What do you need to know about computer models?
- How can business planning lessons be applied to not-for-profit organizations?
- How can managers apply lessons of planning experience to the planning of their own careers?

You don't have to get an advanced degree to make strategic planning a part of your management style. All you need is the expert advice in this idea-packed handbook. (As a bonus, the book includes a glossary of the terms, tools, and techniques of strategic planning.)
8. Finally, John Petersen (2008) has written a book worthy of reading for all those engaged in organizational, departmental, or personal strategic planning, entitled *A Vision for 2012: Planning for Extraordinary Change*. This book is about helping people make sense of the crises on the horizon, and it is also about making organizations and individuals ready for this extraordinary change (Petersen, as adapted from p. 3).

Education

Strategic planning emerged in public education as a management tool in the mid-1980s. The term appeared in educational publications for the first time around 1984, and by 1987 an estimated five hundred school districts around the country were using some type of strategic planning (Conley, 1992).

Two professional organizations, the American Association of School Administrators (AASA) and the Association for Supervision and Curriculum Development (ASCD), promoted strategic planning in education through publishing and widely disseminating two strategic planning handbooks written by national consultants Shirley McCune (*Strategic Planning for Educators*, 1986) and Bill Cook (*Strategic Planning for America's Schools*, 1988).

McCune and Cook proceeded to lead strategic planning workshops for educators around the country under the sponsorship of the two associations, with Cook graduating over four hundred "certified strategic planners" from his AASA-approved program. Educational Leadership, the professional organ of the ASCD, dedicated its April 1991 issue to strategic planning. Today, the Educational Resources Information Center (ERIC) lists over 340 titles written since 1989 under the subject of "strategic planning," which address strategic planning in a variety of educational settings, including schools, universities, and libraries . . .

One comprehensive text on the subject published in the 1990s is *Strategic Planning in Education: Rethinking, Restructuring, and Revitalizing* by Roger Kaufman and Larry Herman. . . . This book "presents a clear picture of the process of strategic planning from start to finish.

This process includes selecting desired results, identifying a mission, assessing needs in order to formulate new purposes, developing and implementing action plans, and evaluating the success of the strategic plan. *Strategic Planning in Education* explains each step of the strategic planning process with lucid examples, and an extensive number of figures, tables, diagrams, matrices, and templates complement the text.

Kaufman and Herman offer practical guidelines, concrete techniques, and pragmatic advice throughout their book, and their hands-on approach towards strategic planning is geared explicitly to an audience of educational practitioners. . . ." (Miech, 1995)

Schools in America are faced with increasing demands and diminishing resources. Rapid social change, increasing diversity, and demands for accountability characterize the education landscape. Schools are expected to change to meet new needs of society and the workplace.

At the same time, these schools have limited resources available to meet these new demands. Support from public sources is not likely to be sufficient to provide the resource base necessary to create and operate the schools of the future. It is, therefore, incumbent on schools throughout the nation to look for sources of funding to supplement those received from public sources or from tuition income raised to support private schools.

One resource written by Adsit and Murdock (2011), *Cutting Costs and Generating Revenues in Education*, is very practitioner-oriented and gives hundreds of proven ways from the field of education to cut costs and several case studies focused on strategic planning that provide sources of additional funding not dependent solely on property taxes or other public funding sources.

This book is a must-read for those wishing to cut costs or generate revenues in education, including school board members; superintendents; business managers; principals; legislative and educational policy makers at the local, state, and national levels; certified and classified staff; parent groups; state level administrator organizations; and national-level administrator, teacher, school board, and parent-teacher organizations.

During the past two decades, institutions of higher education and school districts had to confront numerous changes in their external and internal environment and respond to emerging challenges such as decreasing financial support and rapid technological advances including distance learning, changing demographics, and outdated academic programs. As a result, many universities and school districts engaged in strategic planning as means to "make beneficial, strategic changes . . . to adapt to the rapidly shifting environment" (Rowley, Lujan, and Dolence, 1997).

Overall, strategic planning at universities and school districts has been only moderately successful, as only a few were able to achieve significantly successful results and "transfor[m] themselves dramatically. Others have been able to make important changes in parts of their operations. . . . But many institutions have stumbled, dissolved into controversy, or lost their nerve" (Rowley, Lujan, and Dolence, 1997). Although several authors have endeavored to explain successes and failures of strategic planning in education, scholars differ in their opinions. As a result, there is no consensus (or clarity) on major determinants of strategic planning's success in education.

In fact, in the midst of a brief "overview of strategic planning, there seems to be no evidence that strategic planning actually improves education performance within schools . . . (however), strategic planning can play an important public relations role in education. For example, strategic planning in education can help improve school-community relations by involving parents and community members in the formal strategic planning process" (Miech, 1995, pp. 3-4).

In a 1993 content analysis of seventy-nine strategic plans collected from school districts around the country, David Conley, a professor at the University of Oregon, found that "community relations" was the most frequently cited objective (appearing in 41 of the 79 strategic plans), and he concluded that "strategic planning does seem to be a useful tool for communicating across traditional boundaries between schools and communities. The high recurrence of strategies that address partnerships, public relations, and securing financial resources indicates the importance of this political dimension of the planning process" (1993, p. 25).

In fact, broad modifications in the strategic planning process by educators appear to have facilitated improved school-community relations. In emphasizing the "participatory aspects" of strategic planning and using it as a "public relations tool," educators have changed strategic planning into something quite unlike strategic planning in business, according to Conley: "The descriptions of strategic planning in education are so different from its use in the private sector as to raise the issue of whether the educational model has diverged so far that it deserves some new name" (1992, p. 52).

Miech notes,

> Whereas business often focused strategic planning around relatively detached groups of "experts" within the organization, educators engaging in strategic planning have apparently decided to emphasize the political dimensions of the process in order to increase the number of stakeholders in the school enterprise. This formulation of strategic planning, with its appeal to diverse interests and diffuse distribution of power, increases the likelihood of community involvement in schools, but it also creates problems with ensuring a coordinated focus and a suitable role for expert knowledge. (1995, p.4)

As Conley states:

> Strategic planning attempts to walk a delicate line between interactive/political elements of planning that demand broad-based participation and agreement on general principles and goals, and rationalist elements that require adequate detail and measures to ensure plan implementation. The planning process, with its emphasis on global perspective and consensus decision making, tends to produce rather general statements of intent. . . . The broad goals and intentions appear to lose something in the translation into specific activities designed to transform educational practices, and the result is a series of distinct, often unconnected, educational improvement activities. (1993, p. 26)

Chapter Three

Strategic Planning for Extraordinary Change in the New Information Age, Global Economy of the Twenty-First Century

When the rate of change outside the organization, exceeds the rate of change inside, the organization dies.

—Jack Welch

You never change things by fighting the existing reality. To change something, build a new model that makes the existing model obsolete.

—R. Buckminster Fuller

Globally, we are experiencing an era of extraordinary change. For example, the United States and the rest of the world are experiencing what Petersen (2008) refers to as energy stress; economic stress; demographic stress; environmental stress; climate stress; geopolitical stress; evolutionary stress; governance, financial, and social stress; biotechnological change; changes in artificial intelligence; extraordinary acknowledge access and rapid communications; production innovations; and societal changes—and the list could go on and on.

Strategic planning in a time of extraordinary change and instability is challenging for educational leaders, to say the least. Instead of planning for ten to twenty years in the future using traditional linear models of strategic planning as we did in the past, today successful school districts are planning for anywhere from one to seven years in the future with scenario and contingency planning models being integrated into action plans and used more frequently than in the past.

School leaders are realizing that most human beings don't deal well with discontinuities and rapid change. As Peterson (2008) points out,

> We build our perspectives and options around the past, not generally informed about potential futures. Our underlying values and judgments are all products of

experiences that are quite different from the future arrayed before us. Scientists have estimated that technology and knowledge is exploding a million times faster than the rate at which our underlying social and cognitive frameworks change. . . . (We make) vain attempts to make sense of cutting-edge breakthroughs through the lens of ideas, values, and concepts that are sometimes centuries old (especially in education). (Petersen, 2008)

Jurinski has defined strategic planning "as a process of creating forward-directed long-term objectives for your organization" (1993). Drucker has suggested that "strategic planning is the continual process of making entrepreneurial (risk-taking) decisions systematically and with the greatest knowledge of their futurity, organizing systematically the efforts needed to carry out these decisions, and measuring the results of these decisions against the expectations through systematic feedback (1973).

Others, such as Austin, suggest that strategic planning is best accomplished when cross-institutional plans are tied to the mission of the organization, involve a large number of stakeholders, are data driven, and emerge from an arena of consensus that is heterarchical in leadership (2002).

There is no single definition for strategic planning that covers all organizations in a time of extraordinary change; however, most processes and forms of strategic planning contain at least the common elements of a predetermined process, collaboration on process and outcome implementation, and a system for analyzing and evaluating vision, mission, core values and beliefs, and goals.

Common to most strategic planning models is a process for examining data for both the internal and external environments, including a situational analysis of the internal strengths and weaknesses and the external threats and opportunities. Situational analyses in educational organizations can be conducted on markets, competition, demographics, technology, facility management, food service management, transportation management, financial resources, and human resources, as well as any other significant factors that influence the success of the organization.

Once the school district's situation is analyzed, the organization's strategic planners begin to discuss alternative goals that will strategically place the district into a position of competitive advantage. These actions are then evaluated and selected for implementation by examining them in light of the district's purpose, vision, mission, and values, as well as prioritizing them according to their potential for strategic success.

Strategic planning in school districts typically results in a formal, written, structured strategic plan that charts the organization's future for a specified number of years. As Jurinski points out, a distinction should be made between the strategic planning process and the subsequent strategic plan. The two terms are not synonymous, and it is important to know that this activity traditionally has required both a formal process and written plans (Jurinski, 1993).

Strategic plans in school districts are often implemented through the establishment of detailed accountability mechanisms. Many plans are never fully implemented because of a series of management errors or omissions in the planning process, which might include a failure to develop effective communication channels with those who are responsible for carrying out the plan, failure to use the best data for the situational analysis, or the incorrect analysis of existing data. Many school districts do not understand the actual costs associated with implementing the goals that are identified, or the superintendent fails to support the plan, or he or she creates an atmosphere in which central office and building managers believe that involvement in the communication about the strategic planning process is privileged.

As Austin suggests, some businesses (districts) fail at planning because they do not undertake the process; rather, they borrow the plan of another school district of similar size and composition. They mistakenly believe that they have engaged in a best practice or benchmarking model; thus, they never benefit from the communication, learning, or strategic decision-making that proper planning provides them. Other organizations get so caught up in the process, the data, and the reporting (to the Board and the public) that they fail to develop an effective plan (Austin, 2002) (parenthetical text is mine).

Likewise, Austin states,

> Most plans fail for one or more of the following reasons: 1) inadequate financial resources, 2) inadequate accountability system, 3) strict hierarchical structures that limit implementation, 4) unrealistic timelines, or 5) failure to empower staff and integrate planning into their work life. These reasons emerge mainly in situations of poor leadership, inadequate management, insufficient training, and a general failure to recognize the increasing complexity of the new economy and its influence on the work and family life of our society. (Austin, 2002, p. 10)

THE CURRENT STATUS OF STRATEGIC PLANNING IN SCHOOL DISTRICTS

Strategic planning is now a staple fixture of the American school district landscape, yet few school organizations plan effectively. Many school districts and the enterprises they operate within themselves have passed the point of questioning the need for strategic planning and have entered an era of doubting the validity and reliability of current planning mechanisms.

School district strategic planning efforts are often futile not only for the reasons (Austin, 2002) mentioned above, but also because many school districts are unable to produce tangible results by using measurable performance indicators or to realize the majority of their goals and objectives. The process of strategic planning as implemented by many school districts is far too slow in an age of technological revolution and satisfaction or customer service-on-demand.

Current school leaders often are unable to visualize the urgency of implementing the plans they have envisioned because of their disdain for or inability to make the tough but necessary choices and decisions that emerge as part of the strategic planning process. Many school districts are unable to realize the goals of their strategic plan because their leaders entered the process in "bad faith," and with a preconceived destination or hidden agenda already in mind unrelated or unrevealed to their respective followers.

Those school districts that have been successful in the strategic planning process have several variables in common. First, their superintendent and key leaders are able to envision a shared future and to inspire and motivate others to follow them in the journey to achieve this vision. Second, the superintendent is a professional change agent who has communicated her or his vision of the organizational transformation to the entire district, while ensuring that all members of the staff have a place in its future.

The successful school leaders not only have the ability to forecast the future, but also possess the ability to communicate this future to others. They realize the need for an organizational paradigm shift and they envision the ultimate outcome, communicate it to others, and inspire others into action by creating an atmosphere and sense of urgency. These school district leaders place people, financial resources, infrastructure, and the organizational culture up for discussion and change. Truly inspirational school leaders use urgency and accountability to motivate, and they build an organization based around trust and integrity.

Most school districts currently entering the strategic planning process suffer from two related problems. First, the superintendent leadership style types described above do not currently head unsuccessful organizations, and second, these leaders are not aware of the transformation that our society has been going through over the past thirty-five years.

Our society has entered a state of continuous change, continual disorder, ands increasing levels of differentiation. The only constant is change. This continuous change and the emergently complex levels of differentiation experienced in our current twenty-first-century society confound school districts of every type and size.

Many school districts leap forward into strategic planning without a sound foundation of data, a well-defined plan or a clear expectation of the outcomes expected. Many districts failed to plan strategically. Leaders did not review their plans against the district's mission. By losing sight of the district's mission and purpose, these organizations were unable to distinguish a sound idea from an educational fad, a mere educated guess, or a coming disaster.

Finally, these unsuccessful school districts in regards to strategic planning did not relate their plans to reality, they failed to understand the power of societal transformation on the organization, and they neglected to develop goals in reference to internal and external factors that directly influenced the long-term success of their operation.

CHAPTER SUMMARY

Thus, in strategic planning for extraordinary change in the new information age, global economy of the twenty-first century, it has become a cliché to suggest that we have entered an era of continuously interesting, challenging, and changing times with technological breakthroughs and advancements spiraling out of control. Kennedy (1993) has suggested that the combination of the global population explosion and technological revolutions have created a situation where people, organizations, and nations will fall into one of two categories: winners or losers.

As distance becomes less important, the individual and the family—as well as our methods for understanding and explanation, such as religion, science, and education—are entering an era of unprecedented transformation. Across the globe, our societies and social relations are realigning, organizations are being continuously restructured, and governments are being reconstituted, causing the rigid command-and-control hierarchies to crumble as the center-based power systems of the past move toward shifting dynamic power systems (Knoke, 1996). One only has to consider the recent governmental changes in the Middle East during 2010 and 2011 to attest to that fact.

As Austin points out, our current society is global, diversified, and based within a free market context. This social transformation was brought about by a move toward a knowledge-based system in which technological innovation is rewarded with massive wealth and prestige. For the first time in human history, a social transformation occurred through the diffusion of knowledge and ideology alone. Access to education has been expanded exponentially, religious belief systems are becoming ultra-tolerant to accept an increasing number of viewpoints (with notable exceptions that bring unprecedented global reactions), and our business structures are moving from hierarchical and rule-driven to hyper-diffuse, lateral, flat, increasingly complex, or heterarchical. Planning and business relations have become more complex, more fluid, and more dynamic (Austin, 2002).

The question for future superintendents, central office administrators, department leaders, and school leaders is whether they will choose to create phenomenal, influential, and increasingly prosperous school organizations that continuously improve student learning and achievement, or will simply overlay our past practices of unionization, command-and-control management, and limiting hierarchy over our new economy-based enterprises. Let this author suggest that the school districts that do the latter should begin planning for their demise and ultimate consolidation or bankruptcy.

Judy and D'Amico (1997) provide evidence that suggests that the workforce of the future will need to change and learn to master the changing economic and workplace landscape. They have demonstrated that five distinct forces will shape the American economy over the next twenty years: technological innovation, globalization, economic growth in developing nations, deregulation and liberalization, and shifting demographics.

School organizations that strategically plan within the context of these forces and develop systems to assist their employees to adapt to these factors will emerge at the forefront of their respective competitors. These forces will undoubtedly create a new set of challenges and opportunities for both the school districts and their employees of the future.

Strategically planning in school districts in the future will require districts and their leaders to understand the evolution of the economy and all of the elements of our society. The new economy will require systems that renew current leaders and prepare prospective leaders, while increasing levels of empowerment throughout the organization.

School districts will need tactics, strategies, and mechanisms that continuously advance the skills of their existing students and staff, while simultaneously developing workplace practices that encourage the current employees to remain with the district. Successful school districts of the future will manage their processes and structures, leading their followers toward new mental models and paradigms. New paradigms will shift the school and district's culture toward one of continual adaptation and transformational orientations.

Past systems and practices of strategic planning will become increasingly ineffective and obsolete. Managing change will require a new mechanism for organizational development and leadership practice. As Austin suggests, the successful organizations of the future will produce synergy between the three levels of the enterprise (organizational/global, departmental/local, and personal/individual). To succeed in the aspiration of synergy for the organization, leadership practice, reward systems, and the institutional culture will simultaneously require improvements in theory, practice, and process (2002).

Chapter Four

Brief Case Study Examples of Effective Strategic Plans in the Field of Education

Strategic planning is worthless—unless there is first a strategic vision.

—John Naisbitt

The following represent effective strategic plan examples from the author's personal experience. Each plan was tailored to the particular district's challenges and needs. These plans were effective and drafted by this author after input from all district stake holders (board, administrative, confidential, certified, and classified staff, parents, students, business representatives, community members at large), and consultants used such as state-level school board association PR personnel, legal counsel, local superintendents and the ESD superintendent, legislative representatives, and professional strategic planning facilitators and consultants.

1. Perrydale School District No. 21, Amity, Oregon—Strategic Plan to Survive and Thrive as a Quality Small School of Excellence, 1991–97
2. Crane Elementary and Crane Union High School Strategic Plans, Crane, Oregon
3. Mary M. Knight School District Strategic Plan, Elma (Matlock), Washington

CASE STUDY EXAMPLE #1

Perrydale School District No. 21, Perrydale, Oregon

Strategic plans for generating alternative sources of revenue must be designed to fit the unique needs of the district you are serving at the time. For example, when Tim Adsit served as the superintendent in Perrydale School District No. 21 in Perrydale, Oregon from 1991–1997, they developed the following strategic plan that was successful in increasing district revenues by over $860,000, cutting costs by over $60,000, and placing the district in a more stable financial position after tax limitations had almost caused it to declare bankruptcy:

- Focus the district on the mission of continually improving student learning, achievement, and excellence;
- Lobby local legislators to draft new legislation to increase school funding without increasing property taxes;
- Establish an education foundation;
- Implement a four-day weekly class schedule;
- Conduct a cost reduction study and implement the good ideas generated;
- Write grants;
- Expand the district's student population (which works well in states that have ADMw formulas for funding basic school support);
- Restructure schooling to expand the curriculum without expanding the staff by implementing distance learning and computer instruction technologies.
- Establish school/business partnerships that raise revenues or increase resources and that are mutually beneficial to the district and the business partner;
- Share costs and services with various districts and agencies including parks and recreation districts through consortiums and developing interagency agreements to provide personnel and services at the school site in exchange for use of school facilities when not in use by school students or personnel;
- Plan, develop, and implement various entrepreneurial enterprises and student-run businesses that help to pay for some or all of the class- and student-run business; and
- Stay in a continuous process of school improvement, strategic planning, and change, focused on your mission and on increasing revenues and reducing costs.

CASE STUDY EXAMPLE #2

The following are sample strategic plans for generating alternative revenues developed while serving as the Superintendent of Schools in Crane Union High School District No. 1J and Crane Elementary School District No. 4, Crane, Oregon, between 2001 and 2006:

Adopted Strategic Plan to Generate Alternative Sources of Revenue for Crane Union High School District No. 1J

1. Total commitment to excellence through increased efficiency, accountability, service, employee training, increased parent involvement, and service to gain higher student achievement and mastery of the new basics for the twenty-first century.
2. Lobby our legislators at both the state and federal level for new funds. For example, county roads funds must now be used as an offset against State School Fund revenue support. Encourage our federal legislators to get this bill changed at the federal level so these funds can be used in addition to state school support. Continue lobbying our legislators in regard to many forms of legislation that will either increase revenue or assist in cutting expenses in our schools.
3. Establish a Crane Area Schools Education Foundation, which will allow people and businesses to donate money, goods, or services and receive tax write-offs for doing so. Private funds raised by this foundation could be used to help offset revenue losses from public funds and help us preserve excellence in Crane education. The boards in both districts have already implemented this proposal.
4. Conduct a study and implement agreed-upon recommendations for cost savings that are feasible. The staffs in both districts have already implemented this proposal.
5. Write grants to attract alternative revenue sources. Such grants can be written by the district, the foundation, or both.
6. Utilize all appropriate forms of technology to deliver instruction in different ways. Restructure schooling and the delivery of instructional services, as we currently know them, through full utilization of technology and full implementation of Oregon's Education Act for the Twenty-First Century. Not only maintain our current accreditation status with the state and with the Northwest Association of Schools and Colleges, but also become a model 21st Century School site that receives local, state, national, and international recognition.
7. Establish school-business partnerships and entrepreneurial enterprises both on and off the school site that generate income and job sites for Crane students in grades 7–12. Use some of the profit generated by these programs to help fund the operational expenses of the program.
8. Share costs and services with local area districts, the ESD, a consortium of districts, county and state agencies, the business sector, and higher education while still maintaining Crane Union High School District's identity and autonomy.

9. Conduct further study and gain public input on the concept of voting to develop a small parks and recreation district for the full funding of such high school programs as arts, crafts, and wood shop, music, outdoor education, interscholastic athletics, performing arts, vocational agriculture, and home economics.

    Such a recreation district is capable of utilizing the boundaries of the CUHS district for taxing itself anywhere from $0 up to $10.00 per thousand of assessed valuation. Parks and recreation districts were not limited to $5.00/1000 of assessed valuation under Measure 5, which passed a number of years ago, like schools were.

    This newly formed parks and recreation district would have its own Board of Directors and any employees and programs offered by the newly formed district would be paid from the new district's budget and not from the school district's general fund budget. Another way to accomplish this would be for the newly formed parks and recreation district to enter into an interagency agreement with the CUHS district to pay for these services with the programs and employee's staying at the school. This is the method used in Morrow County School District, Morrow County, Oregon, for example.

    Basically, the formation of such a parks and recreation district would give local taxpayers a way around the limitations of Measure 5 [an Oregon tax limitation initiative] and it would restore some degree of local control to district taxpayers who are looking for new sources of revenues to support schools.

    This idea still uses increased public tax dollars, but it is a better idea than voting a local school levy in addition to state revenues anticipated to be received, because those revenues have to be used as an offset against school support at the present time unless the law is changed. On the other hand, the revenues generated by the newly formed parks and recreation district are in addition to the school district's current level of funding.

    This proposal would have to go before the Harney County Commissioners who would have to vote to allow such a proposal to be on the ballot using the boundaries of CUHS District as the boundaries for the newly formed parks and recreation district. Give the matter some thought; it has great possibilities for resolving most of the current school revenue problems.

10. Continue to add other ideas for generating alternative revenues not solely dependent on property taxes. Implement these new ideas as the Board, staff, administration, parents, students and public are able to reach consensus on them. Brainstorm now to generate more quality ideas!

Adopted Strategic Plan to Generate Alternative Sources of Revenue, Crane Elementary School District No. 4

1. Total commitment to excellence through increased efficiency, accountability, service, employee training, increased parent involvement, and service to gain higher student achievement and mastery of the new basics for the twenty-first century.
2. Lobby our legislators at both the state and federal level for new funds. For example, county roads funds must now be used as an offset against State School Fund revenue support. Encourage our federal legislators to get this bill changed at the federal level so these funds can be used in addition to state school support. Continue lobbying our legislators in regards to many forms of legislation that will wither increase revenue or assist in cutting expenses in our schools.
3. Establish a Crane Area Schools Education Foundation, which will allow people and businesses to donate money, goods, or services and receive tax write-offs for doing so. Private funds raised by this foundation could be used to help offset revenue losses from public funds and help us preserve excellence in Crane Education. The boards in both districts have already implemented this proposal.
4. Conduct a study and implement agreed upon recommendations for cost savings that are feasible. The staffs in both districts have already implemented this proposal.
5. Write grants to attract alternative revenue sources. Such grants can be written by the district, the foundation, or both.
6. Utilize all appropriate forms of technology to deliver instruction in different ways. Restructure schooling and the delivery of instructional services, as we currently know them, through full utilization of technology and full implementation of Oregon's Education Act for the Twenty-First Century. Not only maintain our current accreditation status with the state and with the Northwest Association of Schools and Colleges, but also become a model 21st Century School site that receives local, state, national, and international recognition.
7. Establish school-business partnerships and entrepreneurial enterprises both on and off the school site that generate income and job sites for Crane students in grades 7–12. Use some of the profit generated by these programs to help fund the operational expenses of the program.
8. Share costs and services with local area districts, the ESD, a consortium of districts, county and state agencies, the business sector, and higher education while still maintaining Crane Elementary School District's identity and autonomy.

9. Continue to add other ideas for generating alternative revenues not solely dependent on property taxes. Implement these new ideas as the board, staff, administration, parents, students and public are able to reach consensus on them. Brainstorm now to generate more quality ideas!

Another strategic planning idea for generating revenues and cutting costs is the concept of "value engineering." Once your strategic plan is in order, enter into the value engineering process whereby other experts literally "second guess" the plan or project. This process invariably leads to huge savings and introduces valuable alternatives and considerations. School districts would be well advised to bring in experts from time to time for a modest fee to "second guess" how they are spending their money and make objective suggestions. It is almost guaranteed that the savings will outstrip the costs by a wide margin.

Also, we are at a time when local control and superintendent control are a thing of the past. We need to find every conceivable partner who will do something for us that will save money and expand service. Schools have not been the most welcoming of places for people who wish to share their thoughts and ideas, whether we admit it or not. Educators like to think of themselves as the local experts. We need to shed that mantle and consider every conceivable idea and suggestion that helps make us more effective and efficient.

As this author stated earlier, we don't have as much of a lack of money problem in public education as we have a lack of creative ideas problem. As educators we must learn to think outside the box and change our paradigms.

CASE STUDY EXAMPLE #3

Mary M. Knight School District No. 311, Strategic Plan, 2008–2015: "Continuous Student Learning in a Caring Environment"

Introduction

A strategic plan, like a map, helps an organization move forward with purpose and direction. In 2002, the Mary M. Knight School District, Elma, Washington, developed a School Improvement Plan to provide direction for its educational program. Over the years, we have updated the plan to address changing needs. This strategic plan serves as an overarching framework for building-level action plans and budget priorities from 2008–2015.

Mission

We, the staff and board of directors, believe that every child has the ability to learn. We believe it is our mission to provide a rich, positive, safe environment in which students and staff members can achieve their highest personal and academic potential. We believe this requires a cooperative partnership among staff members, parents, students, and community members.

Vision

Mary M. Knight's vision is to develop lifelong learners who will be competent future citizens of character for the twenty-first century. We will strive to educate our students for the skills needed in the twenty-first century, exceed state, national, and international standards in our schools, and be considered one of the best schools in the world by 2015.

Cornerstones and Principles

To accomplish our mission and vision, we value these fundamental cornerstones and principles:

- Relationships—Student learning is enhanced by trusting relationships that are built among students, staff, parents, and community members.
- Communications—There is consistent communication between and among teachers of all grades. Everyone is involved and connected, including parents and members of the community, in order to solve problems and create solutions.
- Balance—Everyone should strive to balance school, home, and recreation to improve productivity.
- Focus—The vision is shared and everyone plays a vital role in achieving our vision.
- All children can learn.
- Positive relationships and respect for each individual among the district's diverse cultures are of utmost importance.
- Each child is important and deserves academic success, appropriate challenge, and employment skills for the twenty-first century.
- A student-focused, performance-based education system has the greatest prospect for developing productive members of society.
- Academic, career, and citizenship skills, personal growth, and enhancement of self-worth are instructional responsibilities.
- High expectations are communicated to all students and staff.
- Varied and multiple forms of student assessment based on defined standards ensure fairness and communicate respect for individual learning styles.
- The entire community is part of the educational system.
- Operating under district goals and policy, schools make decisions at the local level.

- A safe, comfortable, positive learning environment conducive to learning is essential.
- Continuous quality improvement of the educational culture and system is critical.
- Emphasis is placed on uninterrupted student instructional time.
- We must move from a reactive orientation focused on problems to a proactive orientation focused on our shared vision.
- We must move from a focus on practice, inputs, and processes to a focus on student performance and outcomes.
- We must move from individual action to collegial action.
- We must move from short-term improvement efforts and goal-setting to sustained, long-term, systematic efforts, and goal-attainment.
- We must move from perception-based decisions to data-based decisions.
- We must move from use of craft knowledge alone to use of research and craft knowledge.
- We must move from individual/district responsibility to school district/school and individual responsibility.
- We must align district budgets with the priorities in this strategic plan.

Student Learning Goals

These goals represent what we want students to learn. They reflect community input and are consistent with the learning goals for the state of Washington. We commit to teach our students to:

- Read with comprehension, write with skill, and communicate effectively and responsibly in a variety of ways and settings.
- Know and apply the core concepts and principles of mathematics; social, physical and life sciences; civics and history; geography; fine arts; and health and fitness.
- Think analytically, logically, and creatively, and integrate experience and knowledge to form reasoned judgments and solve problems.
- Understand the importance of work and how performance, effort, and decisions directly impact career and educational opportunities.
- Be responsible for one's actions; develop positive self-worth and academic success through good work and study habits; show respect for others; participate as a citizen; and become a lifelong learner.

Improvement Targets

- Annually decrease the percentage of students not meeting the standard in reading by 10 percent as measured by the Washington Assessment of Student Learning (WASL).

- Annually decrease the percentage of students not meeting the standard in math by 10 percent as measured by the WASL.
- Increase the percentage of students meeting the standard on the tenth-grade WASL to 70 percent on the first attempt in all three areas—reading, math, and writing—by 2010.
- Each school will close its academic achievement gap by bringing the percentage of students not meeting the standard in reading, math, and writing as measured by the WASL to below the percentage of poverty in that school.

Improvement Goals

- Operate the district as a cohesive K–12 system focused on a shared vision of quality education for all students.
- Maintain high expectations for both students and staff; continue to recruit, select, evaluate, train, and supervise all staff.
- Provide honest and impartial decision-making focusing on the best educational interest of the students.
- Focus on team building and creating a collaborative work environment.
- Work on strengthening positive relationships, communications, and school climate between and among all staff members, the board, and the community.
- Enhance use of technology as a communication, management, and instructional tool for the twenty-first century and maintain an up-to-date technology plan.
- Plan, develop, and implement a year-round communications plan aimed at both internal and external audiences to help inform, improve communications, and unify staff and voters.
- Over the next five to seven years, plan, develop, implement, and evaluate curriculum and programs according to a newly revised district/state curriculum adoption cycle utilizing current research and data-based decision-making models and aligning all district curriculums K–12 to state Essential Academic Learning Standards (EALRs), Grade Level Expectations (GLEs), national, and international standards.
- Work with the community and staff to make a facility plan and implement it. Immediately develop a long-range facilities plan involving the community, parents, staff, and students in the planning process in appropriate and timely ways, implement the plan, and henceforth annually update the plan. Continuously plan, develop, implement, manage, and evaluate an effective program of supervision of buildings, grounds, protective maintenance, and operation of the school facilities.

Listed below are specific areas in which we will take immediate action to ensure that our goals are met.

Support Strategies

As a professional learning community, we will pursue a collaborative investigation of how we can together achieve our mission, vision, improvement targets and improvement goals.

Curriculum, Instruction, and Assessment

We have a commitment to a continuous cycle that aligns and connects curricula delivered through quality instructional practices and materials that will produce excellence as measured by a variety of common assessments. We will:

- Align district curriculum, instruction, and assessment with Grade Level Expectations to improve student achievement.
- Provide targeted assistance by using assessment data to identify student needs and appropriate strategies.
- Allocate and utilize resources based on student needs and School Improvement Plans.
- Provide ongoing professional development for aligned curriculum, assessment, and instructional best practices.
- Use assessment results to improve student performance and instructional programs.
- Promote an understanding of the relevancy of education and its connection to the workplace by providing opportunities for all students to participate in career- and work-based activities.

Safe and Inclusive Environment

Our students, staff and parents will feel safe, supported, and valued within our school community. We will:

- Collect data and examine the results to create specific goals.
- Develop appropriate goals to increase the number of students, staff, and parents who feel safe, supported and valued.

Parent and Community Involvement

We provide opportunities for parent and community involvement as they participate in the continuous improvement of student learning. We will:

- Promote parent and community involvement at each building.
- Communicate expectations, needs, and available opportunities for parent and community involvement.

- Support parent and community participation with communication, finances, policy, and training.
- Maintain partnerships with parents, community, and local businesses.

Organizational Structure and Processes

We will be an organization whose structures and processes are aligned to promote a collaborative, district-wide approach to decision-making that supports quality teaching and learning. We will:

- Promote continuous learning for students, staff, and parents.
- Use research-based practices and carefully formulated action plans to achieve our vision.
- Involve all stakeholders through a participatory planning process to create programs and strategies to most effectively serve our students today and in the future.
- Value and structure the organization to promote extensive communication, cooperation, and collaboration between school staff, parents, and community members.
- Commit to ongoing instructional improvement.

Parameters

We will accomplish our commitment to provide "Continuous Student Learning in a Caring Environment" within the following parameters:

- We will maintain a safe and positive school environment with a commitment to student learning.
- We will abide by laws, district policies, administrative rules, and contractual agreements.
- We will maintain responsible fiscal and resource management practices. The district will budget an unrestricted fund balance of at least 7 percent of the previous year's general fund expenditure budget. The Board of Directors may authorize a "restricted" fund balance above the 7 percent for specific purposes such as capital projects, contingencies, textbooks, and technology.

Guiding Principles

New issues, initiatives, or current practices will be evaluated using the following principles:

- Is it educationally sound and consistent with the strategic plan?
- Will the public support it?

- Are resources available?
- Can it be done legally?

If the answer is *YES* to all of these questions, then we should consider doing it. If we are unsure about any of the above, additional research may be appropriate. If the answer is *NO* to any of the above, other options will be considered.

Get Involved

We welcome the involvement of parents and community members interested in helping the district further achieve its commitment to provide "Continuous Student Learning in a Caring Environment." If you have questions about this strategic plan, are interested in volunteering or would like more information, contact your local school, the district office, or visit our website.

Our Schools

Mary M. Knight Junior-Senior High School
2987 W. Matlock Brady Rd.
Elma, WA 98541-9713
(360) 426-6767

Mary M. Knight Elementary School
2987 W. Matlock Brady Rd.
Elma, WA 98541-9713
(360) 426-6767

Chapter Five

The Process and Tools for Organizational and Departmental Strategic Planning in Education

Goals are SMART . . . Specific, Measurable, Achievable, Realistic, and Timely.

—Unknown

In this short chapter, this author has chosen to refer you to chapter 4 of Austin's book (pages 39–51), which is entitled, "The Art of Triadic Strategic Planning (Institutional, Departmental, and Personal)." Of all the literature reviewed by this author in preparation for writing this book, Austin's description of the process and tools for organizational and departmental or team strategic planning, seems the best. You are encouraged to also buy a copy of his book as well, as it is a useful reference (Austin, 2002).

As mentioned earlier by Austin, in his new planning process, which he calls triadic heterarchical strategic planning, he suggests that all executives and staff should be given greater decision-making power and a larger sphere of influence through the planning process than was given and stressed in traditional models. He goes on to demonstrate that power and influence are guided by principles of trust and responsibility when the emphasis is on collaboration and "win-win" outcomes.

His new model shows that an emphasis on quality is of paramount importance in the development of an organizational planning and outcomes model where measurements of success emphasize integrated institutional, departmental, and personal outcomes over the planning process (Austin, 2002).

As the three-level planning process is implemented in school systems, Austin goes on to say, "leaders are asked to implement a system of personal goal development and evaluation that unites the focus of institutional and departmental values with those of the staff. This creates a system that is more heterarchical and more likely to develop a shared vision and a system of shared responsibility that is often publicly expressed and sought" (Austin, 2002, p. 39).

Austin goes on to say, "This new model is dramatically different from traditional models of strategic planning that emphasize the conventional hierarchy, command and control, and the development of plans through a standard systemic process. In this sort of planning, brainstorming is key and the central decision for leaders is whether the plan should occur every year, every three years, or every five years" (Austin, 2002, p. 4).

The individual who has developed his or her own personal strategic plan and aligned it with the school, department, or district must incorporate the visions of leadership into everyday practice. It is important for district and school management to realize the necessity of integrating the ideas of individual employees into both the short and long-range strategic planning model.

Thus, the goal is an integrated district-wide strategic planning process as is being suggested above. At the organizational/district planning level the outcome goals are: 1) common vision, mssion, and goals; 2) analysis of district data; 3) identification of alternative strategies; 4) increased organizational effectiveness; and 5) district-wide culture change.

At the departmental and/or school level, the outcome goals are: 1) integration of mission and goals; 2) analysis of departmental or school data; 3) identification of alternative strategies; 4) increased departmental or school effectiveness; and 5) departmental or school-wide culture change.

At the team and/or personal strategic planning level, the outcome goals are: 1) integration of mission and goals; 2) analysis of life accomplishments; 3) identification of personal goals; 4) personal Success; and 5) attitude and productivity improved in all aspects of life and career, business, or profession.

Likewise, in *A Guide to Planning for Change*, Norris and Poulton emphasize the importance of institutional context—and organizational support—in shaping any planning effort. Educational institutions and departments are complex organizations. No single planning style or approach can suit every situation. Organizations vary widely with respect to the nature and complexity of their institutional missions, and with respect to their size, control or governance, and the presence or absence of collective bargaining agreements.

Planning is a core competency of successful organizations, leaders, and managers. It pervades all organizational units and processes. Educational planning in all its forms engages a broad cross-section of administrative leaders, staff, faculty, students, parents, community members, alumni, and other stakeholders. Planning is ongoing, on different time frames and schedules (Norris and Poulton, p. 1).

POINTS TO REMEMBER

- Power and influence are guided by principles of trust and responsibility when the emphasis is on collaboration and "win-win" outcomes.
- An emphasis on quality is of paramount importance in the development of an organizational planning and outcomes model where measurements of success emphasize integrated institutional, departmental, and personal outcomes over the planning process.
- It is the individual who has developed his/her own personal strategic plan and aligned it with the school, department, or district who must incorporate the visions of leadership into everyday practice. It is important for district and school management to realize the necessity of integrating the ideas of individual employees into both the short and long-range strategic planning model.
- No single planning style or approach can suit every situation. Organizations vary widely with respect to the nature and complexity of their institutional missions, and with respect to their size, control or governance, and the presence or absence of collective bargaining agreements.
- Planning is a core competency of successful organizations, leaders, and managers. It pervades all organizational units and processes. Educational planning in all its forms engages a broad cross-section of administrative leaders, staff, faculty, students, parents, community members, alumni, and other stakeholders. Planning is ongoing, on different time frames and schedules.

Chapter Six

The Process and Tools for Personal Strategic Planning

By failing to prepare, you are preparing to fail.

—Benjamin Franklin

In this chapter, the process and tools for personal strategic planning are presented. *You are encouraged to develop your own personal strategic plan in a separate three-ring binder, notebook, or journal.*

Below is the author's comprehensive personal strategic plan example which includes the following steps:

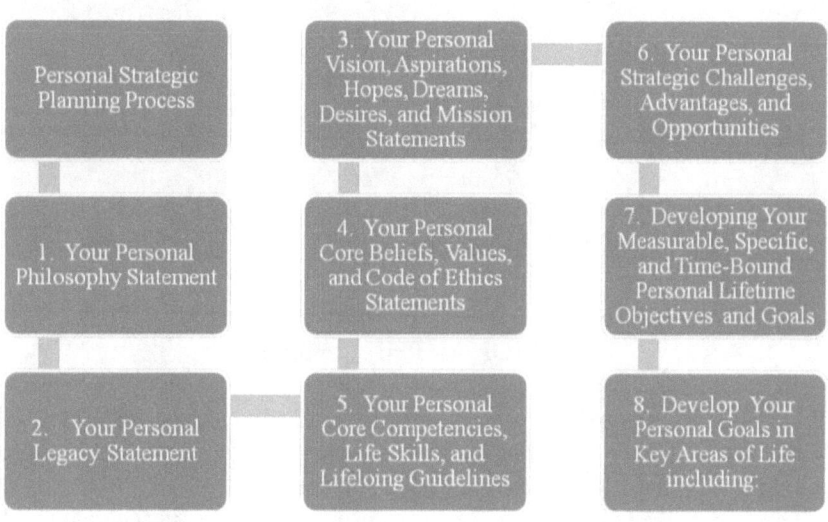

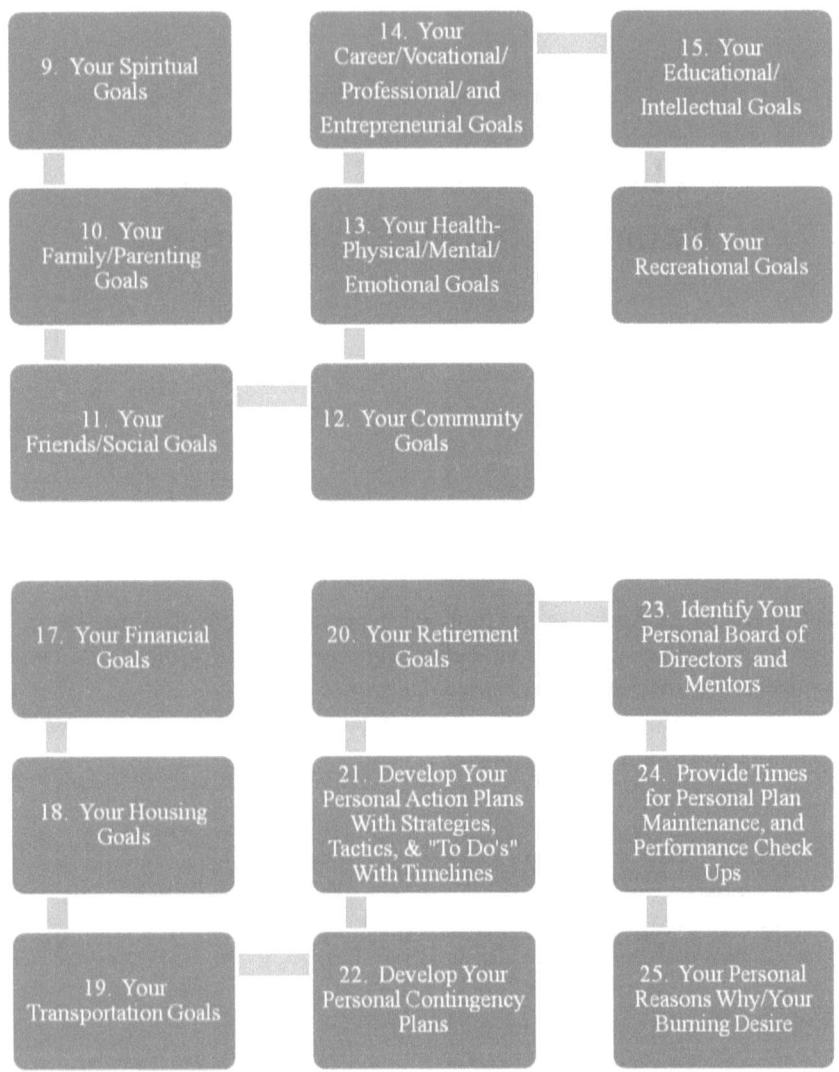

PERSONAL PHILOSOPHY

What is your personal philosophy statement? Everyone has some kind of personal philosophy consisting of some rules adopted from parents, culture, religion, teachers, friends, relatives, acquaintances, etc.

Directions: Write it down in short sentences or in a list on a separate sheet of paper.

This author's personal philosophy example includes the following:

A. "Seek ye first the kingdom of God and his righteousness; and all these things shall be added unto you." Matthew 6:33 (KJV)
B. You can have anything in life that you want, if you help enough other people get what they want.
C. The way to be a success is to find a need and to fill it.
D. Success is the progressive realization of a worthwhile goal or dream that is not against man's laws or God's laws.
E. Do unto others as you would have them do unto you.
F. Work as if it all depends on me, but pray knowing that it all depends on God.

LEGACY STATEMENT

What is your legacy statement, what do you want to be remembered for?
This author's legacy statement example:

I desire to be remembered as a good Christian who shared the Gospel with others and won some souls for Christ, who was a loving and faithful husband to my wife, who tried to be a loving, caring, and nurturing father and grandfather to my children and grandchildren, who helped them grow and develop into responsible citizens, who was goal-oriented and driven from birth to be the best scholar, athlete, teacher, school administrator, consultant, author, lay pastor, and independent business owner he could be, and who continued to be of service to others and to work toward achieving his lifetime goals and objectives until the day he died and went to Heaven.

MISSION STATEMENT

What is your mission statement? A mission statement is a declaration of who you are, why you exist, and what you intend to accomplish in life. What is your life's business? What is your reason for living?

As a Christian, the author's personal mission is to help fulfill the Great Commission found in the Bible which states, "Go ye therefore, and teach all nations, baptizing them in the name of the Father, and of the Son, and of the Holy Ghost: Teaching them to observe all things whatsoever I have commanded you: and, lo, I am with you alway, even unto the end of the world." Matthew 28:19–20 (KJV). This author endeavors to do this in several ways, such as witnessing to others when the occasion arises, supporting God's work (particularly through financial support of missions and through religious and inspirational writing and poetry), and living a Christian way of life in day-to-day action with others.

CORE VALUES

What are your core values? What are your guidelines and measurements for value-centered living? Write them down.

The author's core values, lifelong guidelines, and life skills include:

> Leading a Christ-Centered Life, Growing Responsible Citizens, Trustworthiness, Truthfulness, Striving for Your Personal Best, Active Listening, No Put-Downs With Respect to Other People, Being a Leader and Positive Role Model, Caring, Common Sense, Cooperation, Courage, Curiosity, Effort, Flexibility, Friendship, Initiative, Integrity, Organization, Patience, Perseverance, Pride in Performance, Problem-Solving, Resourcefulness, Responsibility, Sense of Humor, Time Management, Hard Worker, and Smart.

CODE OF ETHICS

What is your code of ethics? Words influence our attitudes and opinions. Write down your personal codes of conduct, your personal creeds, and personal pledges that reflect your effort to make sense of things, to organize your behavior, and to better understand yourself.

The author's code of ethics example includes the following:

The Ten Commandments

1. Do not worship other gods.
2. Do not worship idols.
3. Do not misuse God's name.
4. Keep the Sabbath holy.
5. Honor your father and mother.
6. Do not murder.
7. Do not commit adultery.
8. Do not steal.
9. Do not lie.
10. Do not covet.

LIFETIME OBJECTIVES

What are your lifetime objectives? Your lifetime objectives should be written within the context and framework of your legacy and mission statements written above. One of the keys to your personal strategic plan is to visualize your desired outcomes in advance. Be sure to write and rewrite, and refine your lifetime objectives as affirmations and affirmation statements of the future you are working to realize and read these statements daily, once after arising in the morning and once before going to bed at night.

The author's lifetime objectives example includes:

1. To be able to help fulfill the Great Commission, share the Gospel, and win souls for Christ through witnessing to others when the occasion arises, supporting God's work (particularly through financial support of missions and through religious and inspirational writing and poetry).
2. To daily be a loving and faithful husband to my wife and to be a loving, caring, and nurturing father and grandfather to my children and grandchildren, and help them grow and develop into responsible citizens.
3. To continue to be of service to others through educational administration consulting, writing, ministering, and expanding my independent businesses in my semi-retirement years.
4. To achieve the realistic goals outlined in this personal strategic plan.

GOALS AND ACTION PLANS

What are your goals and your action plans to carry them out? The keys in writing your goals are to make them measurable, specific, and time-bound. Your goals need to be written for each of the thirteen critical activity areas of life to include: Spiritual; Family/Parenting if you have or want to have children; Friends/Social; Community; Health: Physical, Mental/Emotional; Career/Vocational/Professional; Educational/Intellectual; Recreational; Financial; Housing; and Transportation.

The author's measurable, specific, and time-bound personal goals and action plans to carry them out are attached, as examples, on separate sheets at the end of this chapter.

Directions: You are encouraged to develop your own goals on a separate sheet of paper. Consider staying SMART: Specific, Measurable, Attainable, Realistic and within a specific Timeframe with your goals.

PERSONAL BOARD OF DIRECTORS

Who is on your personal board of directors? Who are your mentors? A personal board will accelerate your progress by providing both wisdom and support for the attainment of a specific purpose.

Directions: Write down the names of your personal board members.

The author's personal board of directors and mentors list example includes twenty-five names. The people's names are omitted herein for privacy and because of editorial space needs, but each reader is encouraged to develop her or his own list.

MAINTENANCE AND PERFORMANCE CHECK-UPS

On a monthly basis, you should schedule a time with yourself to evaluate your performance through maintenance and performance check-ups. Ask yourself questions such as these: What progress I you made? Where have I had challenges? What do I need to do differently or more of? Less of? Are my goals realistic and achievable, or are they unrealistic and unachievable?

PERSONAL REASON WHY

What is your personal reason why? What is your dream, your burning desire that prompted your to develop a personal strategic plan in the first place? You won't become successful until and unless you identify, support, and empower your "reasons why." Your whys provide fuel for achievement, and are the reasons behind all action and/or inaction. The mark of all high achievers is a burning desire and why. They know what they want, how and when they will achieve it, but most importantly they know why they want to become successful at achieving their goals.

Everyone has a definition of success, but one of the best this author has ever heard is that "success is the progressive realization of a worthwhile goal or dream that is not against any of man's laws or God's laws" (Puryear, 1980).

The author's personal reasons why examples include:

> To be a success in life, as defined above, to be of service to God and others here on earth, to give something back and pass what has been learned along to family, friends, and others, to enjoy an abundant Christ-centered life, to share the power of my dreams with like-minded people, to be empowered and help empower others, to always be in a goal-setting and goal achieving process, to reach a state of self-actualization and be "always becoming," to gain the personal satisfaction and recognition that comes from being the best one can be in all areas of life, and to stay in proper alignment putting God first, family second, country third, primary job fourth, secondary jobs or sources of income fifth, and all other activities sixth.

We all need to take time to renew ourselves personally, so we can return to our activities, job, and responsibilities in life refreshed and ready for action in doing our best. And, we need to balance our renewal in the activities and areas of life mentioned above.

Thus, in summary, personal strategic planning is a cyclic, systematic process by which an individual envisions his/her future and develops the necessary procedures and operations to achieve that future including: strategic thinking; identifying your personal philosophy, legacy, vision, aspirations, hopes, dreams, desires, and mission statements; identifying your personal core beliefs, values, and code of ethics; identifying your core competencies, life skills, and lifelong guidelines; identifying your strategic challenges, advantages, and opportunities; developing your measurable, specific, and time-bound personal lifetime objectives and goals in key areas of life including: spiritual, family/parenting if you want to have or have children, friends/social, community, health: physical, mental/emotional, career/vocational/professional, educational/intellectual, recreational, financial, housing, and transportation; developing your action plans with strategies and tactics and your contingency plans; identifying a personal board of directors, times for maintenance and performance check-ups, and your personal reasons why; and in the process becoming truly successful, achieving your life objectives and goals, leaving a significant legacy, and achieving self-actualization and personal satisfaction.

A personal strategic life plan is the passport to your success in continuously improving your learning, performance, achievement, and life goal attainment in all aspects of your life. You are encouraged to use this template and process in developing your own personal strategic plan. The template's purpose is to encourage the reader to participate in developing his or her own personal strategic life plan. This life plan, once completed, will serve as the passport to your success in continuously improving your learning, performance, achievement, and life goal attainment in all aspects of your life, including your job, career, or profession. The plan may be completed in two hours or take as much as two weeks depending on how much you have thought about the things in the plan already and the time you can dedicate to the process at any one sitting.

Strategic planning dates back to the time when ancient Greek warriors planned campaigns for military warfare. The etymology of "strategy" is with the Greeks, who elected a "stratego" (general of the army) to lead the regiment. These men gave the "strategic" advice to win battles and manage wars. Thus "strategic planning" aims at achieving the final result of the plan. The benefits of strategic planning have been understood and adopted by men and women in all walks of life including business, government, education, and health care. Yet it is the military discipline that gets the credit for popularizing this dynamic method of planning. Strategic plans revolve around several main questions and stages:

1. What do you want?
2. What are you willing to give up to get what you want?
3. How do you plan your work?
4. How do you work your plan?

This author has successfully used strategic planning in his career of education and personally throughout life to date. But it is not the corporate, organizational, or departmental type of strategic planning we are concerned with in detail in this book; instead, you are encouraged to plan, develop, and implement your own personal strategic life plan on paper, place it in a three-ring binder, journal, or notebook, and align it or link it to your school district, school, department or team strategic plan.

PERSONAL STRATEGIC PLANNING PROCESS TEMPLATE EXAMPLE

What are your personal values and core beliefs?

Whether you recognize it or not, you have values that govern your values and beliefs. Your core values influence how you make decisions. Your core values reflect what is important to you, how you see the world (your paradigm), and what you believe in.

Directions: On a separate sheet of paper, make a list of the things you value. What are your core values?

Do you have a model for your future?

Do you have a real vision of the future for you and your family over the next ten to fifteen years, complete with written strategies to achieve that vision? Successful businesses and institutions have visions of their future and strategic plans that they not only follow, but monitor and update on a regular basis. This is an effective model that can be applied to personal lives, including your life.

Developing a vision of your future and a personal strategic plan is not a complicated process, but it does take some thought and time. The process starts with personal research that includes an understanding of your life stages, the forces that drive your life and plausible events for your current life stage. The next step is exploring plausible futures with personal scenarios. At that point, you are ready to define a vision of your future then create a plan that will help you achieve that vision.

Your personal vision

What is a personal vision, and how do you define it? A personal vision is simply your statement of what you want your future to be. When asked, some people say that their vision is to be healthy, wealthy, and successful. That's a good start, but you should recognize that those terms might have different meanings at different times in your life. "Healthy" to a young person may mean healthy enough to compete in competitive sports, while someone in their seventies may consider health to mean the absence of illness or the ability to walk moderate distances comfortably. Views or measurements of wealth and success may also vary between individuals and at different stages of life.

DIRECTIONS FOR DEVELOPING YOUR OWN PERSONAL VISION STATEMENT

To develop your vision of the future, start with your paper, notebook, or journal and ask yourself "What?" What do you want for your future? What would your future look like if there were no financial restraints? No time constraints?

Now, ask yourself about your values. What or who is really important in your life? Family? Career? Wealth? Ethics? Knowledge? What do you want to achieve during this life stage? Career advancement? Raise a family? Educate your children? Travel? Accumulate? Change the world?

Summarize all of this into one sentence about your preferred future. Two at the most. This written vision should give you direction, declare where you are going, what you want to achieve and, by implication, what you want to avoid.

Your personal mission

Do you feel that you have a mission in life? This is something different than a vision. This is something that you feel you must accomplish. Not everyone feels they have a mission during each stage of life, but others do. Whether it's to get your children or grandchildren educated, to write a book, to bring about social change, achieve a certain social status or any other mission that is a motivating force in your life, you should write it down, next to your vision of your future.

Are the vision and the mission compatible or are the mutually exclusive? You will have to decide how to resolve any differences, but the important thing here is to recognize how the mission and vision can work together, and how you can reconcile them if necessary and plan to accomplish both in the future.

Directions: Write your personal mission statement on your own paper, notebook, or in your journal.

Directions: Write down your personal short and long-range goals, objectives, and performance indicators in a fashion similar to this on your paper, in your notebook, or journal.

Short Range Goals	*Mid-Range Goals*	*Long-Range Goals*	*Ultimate Life-Goals*
1–2 years	*5 years*	*20 years*	

Spiritual:

Personal:

Health—Physical/Mental/Emotional:

Recreational:

Family/Parenting goals:

Social/Friends:

Civic/Community/State/Nation/World:

Career/Profession:

Financial:

Household:

Educational/Intellectual:

Transportation:

Your personal strategy

With your vision and mission defined, the next step in strategic planning is to devise strategies to achieve your vision. A strategy is simply a way to do something, but some strategies are better than others. Good strategies are what make the difference for winning generals, championship chess players, business owners, or educators. The winners develop better strategies than their opponents.

You may not have an opponent to deal with, but working to improve and fully develop your strategies will improve your likelihood of success. So, for each component of your vision, ask "How?" How will you achieve that component of your vision of the future? What strategy will you use to advance your career? Working harder in your present position? Changing firms? Changing industries? Getting more education? Starting your own business? Any of those strategies may work, but you will have to pick the best combination for your situation.

As you go through the various components of your vision, written and unwritten, you will develop a list of strategies for your career and your family, and others for health, housing, and finances. Some may be relatively short-term strategies, but most will be long-term strategies. For example, decisions to stop smoking, to follow a nutritious diet, to exercise regularly may appear to be short-term strategies, but they are all part of a long-term strategy for good health that will have its biggest payoff well after you reach retirement age.

Directions: On a separate sheet of paper list your personal strategies to achieve your personal vision for the future including personal strategies for the following:

Spiritual:
Personal:
Health/Emotional/Mental/Physical:
Recreational:
Family:
Social/Friends:
Civic/Community/State/National/International/Global:
Career/Professional:
Financial:
Household:
Cultural:

Events in your future life

In addition to strategies to achieve your vision of the future, you should consider life events that are likely to occur in your future. Specifically, you should develop strategies for high probability/high-impact events. In the earlier section about strategies to achieve your preferred future, you considered mostly positive events or achievements, but now you should look at any event that has both a high probability of occurrence and will have a strong impact on your life.

As an adult, one event may be the emergence of teenage children. Another might be the risk of divorce. Both require strategies. In middle age, your children will probably leave home and start their own lives, and you may need a strategy to deal with the impacts of this change. You may find that your parents will need your assistance during this stage due to health problems. You will also want to start preparing for your retirement years. If you are in the independent elder stage, you will need strategies for the time in your future when you or your spouse is not be able to make sound decisions, particularly during a health crisis. For any stage of life, strategies developed in the present can make life in the future move more smoothly during turbulent times.

Try to develop strategies that have some flexibility and feasibility. You should be prepared to modify or change a strategy if it becomes appropriate, and you will not want to be locked into a strategy that is failing.

Directions: List strategies on paper, or in your notebook or journal to deal with probable life events and life cycle stages.

Your personal action plan

When you have decided on your strategies to achieve your vision and to deal with life events, you can start laying out an action plan. This is the portion of your strategic plan that answers the question "When?" Your personal strategic plan should reach ten or fifteen years into the future, usually linked to the end of a life stage. (Infancy: Birth to 18 months; Early Childhood: 18 months to 3 years; Play Age: 3 to 5 years; School Age: 6 to 12 years; Adolescence: 12 to 18 years; Young Adulthood: 18 to 35; Mature Adulthood: 35 to 55–65; Late Adulthood: 55–65 to Death; see http://www.learningplaceonline.com/stages/organize/Erikson.htm). Your action plan will be a isting of actions you want to take each year to implement your strategies for achieving your vision and mission, and for dealing with high-impact life events.

You can approach the construction of your action plan from either direction from the present working toward the future, or from the future working backward to the present. The latter, working backward from a perspective in the future, is a technique used by futurists and is termed "back casting." Whichever approach you take to developing your action plan, the result will be a sequence of actions to be listed and taken over the years.

The action plan should be reviewed frequently, and analyzed to determine 1) if the appropriate actions are being taken and 2) if the strategies are proving effective. You should recognize at the start that the future will not unfold exactly as you have planned it, so you will have to adjust your strategies and your actions as you progress into the future.

There are other futures techniques or methods that can be incorporated into personal strategic planning that can be applied to your personal life. Without pursuing too much detail, you might ask yourself a few questions. What are your vulnerabilities? What one event could completely change your future?

Your strengths? Weaknesses? What opportunities are available? Are there any threats on the horizon? Now or in the future? Are there any gaps between your plan and your capabilities? Can you actually perform the actions you are planning? These thoughts are not intended to undermine your vision of the future, but to recognize reality wherever you must face it, now or later.

Directions: Ask yourself these action planning questions as you begin, and write them done on paper:

What do I need to do more of?
What do I need to do less of?
What do I need to begin doing?
What do I need to stop doing?

Directions: Your personal action plan template should look something like this example. You are encouraged to word-process or sketch out your own personal action plan on a separate sheet of paper, using one, for each goal that requires action:

Goal:
Objectives:
   1.
   2.
   3.

Priority	Action (Tasks)	Due Date	Person Responsible	Results/Progress to Date/Contingencies

Change of plans—If ... then ...

The last step in creating your strategic plan involves designing contingency plans, strategies for dealing with unexpected events, or "wild cards." Futurists use the term "wild cards" in reference to low probability, high impact events. Accidents, fires, and natural disasters are often cited as wild cards, but not all wild cards are negative events. An unexpected financial windfall, multiple births, an unexpected child or grandchild and recognition for your personal or business achievements may also be wild card events.

Contingency plans may rely on "if... then..." strategies: "*If* this happens, *then* I will take this action." In your action plan, you started implementing strategies in advance of an event. In contingency planning, the strategy is executed after the event, although preparation may take place in advance. One example of a strategy to prepare for a wild card event is insurance. Insurance is purchased in advance of the event in order to provide funds to help offset losses and aid recovery from the event.

Directions: For your contingency plan, list on a separate sheet of paper possible wild card events that might occur in your future.

Is your geographic area susceptible to earthquakes, floods, hurricanes or other natural hazards? If so, how will you prepare? Insurance is one possibility, but an evacuation plan for your family may be more important. Can you reinforce your home to withstand unexpected natural forces? Should you have food, water, medical supplies, or equipment available? On a more personal level, what would you do if your spouse suddenly became very ill, or died? Asking yourself questions of this type while constructing your contingency plan will help you think through your strategies and the actions you will take if one of these wild cards occurs.

"*If* this happens, *then* I will take this action."

Your strategic plans for contingencies

Goal:
Objectives:
 1.
 2.
 3.

Priority	Action (Tasks)	Due Date	Person Responsible	Results/Progress to Date/Contingencies

Live your personal plan

The final step in strategic planning may be the most important.... Live your plan!

One of the frustrations that professionals who work in the area of strategic planning with businesses and institutions face is that often an organization will go through the entire strategic planning process, then never execute the plan. Hopefully, by the time you complete your plan you will recognize that you not only have an investment in your plan, but you have the opportunity to improve the future for your family and yourself.

As you live your plan, be sure to monitor how your life is unfolding. Are you living the scenario you expected or sought? Or is another scenario developing? By monitoring all aspects of your life and maintaining an awareness of the world as it changes around you, you should be able to adjust your plan, modify your strategies where necessary, and take your life in the direction that will be most favorable to you and your family. This process of monitoring your progress and changing direction when necessary is very like tacking a sailboat as you sail into the wind. You can alter your course many times while successfully proceeding toward your destination.

Monitor and adjust: live your personal strategic life plan, but monitor your progress and change direction when necessary (as adapted from Verne Wheelwright, www.personalfutures.net/ and www.yourpersonalfuture.blogspot.com/).

TO SUMMARIZE YOUR STRATEGIC LIFE PLAN

Your strategic life plan considers all of the areas in your life that are important to you. This plan is based on a framework of personal values, hopes, and dreams. Straying from your plan on a whim becomes a risk that's quantifiable. So having any plan in place provides a means to calculate risk and manage impulsiveness.

For a high school, community college, or college student this is imperative, as the risks and available impulses are many.

It's just like surfing, snowboarding, skydiving, or bungee jumping. They are exhilarating and sometimes terrifying sports. For a few, calm moments, just before you launch off the top of the wave or that enormous mountain that will propel you into the twists and turns below, or jump from the plane or bridge, you can see almost everything in front of you. At once, you decide how to take the turns, manage the risk, and if you gain too much speed, how to slow down or duck out entirely. The more you practice, the better you get, and the more natural the decision-making feels.

Going through life without a strategic plan would be like a novice snowboarder deciding to blaze down a treacherous course instead of a sensible bunny hill. Imminent disaster might occur.

This template example is meant to help you organize your priorities, establish your life goals and design your own plan on paper.

Step 1: Establish your priorities

List the areas in your life that are very important to you. This list might include your family, career, health, financial security, community service, spiritual aspects, etc. Once you identify your valuable areas, number them from extremely important (#1) to least important (#20, or whatever you ended up with).

Step 2: Establish your goals

For each of your priorities identified in Step 1 above, think about where you want to be in that area of your life in the next one to two years, the next five years, and ultimately, at the end of your life.

My life areas

In 1–2 years I want to be here:
In 5 years I want to be here:
Ultimately, I want to be here:

Step 3: Develop your action plan

Keep this in your mind at all times: What gets planned, gets done! Without specific steps and dates, all you have is a wish list—not a plan. Writing in the details of the plan is essential to your success. This is where you set in place the action steps and deadlines to get you where you want to be and help you accomplish your goals.

Consider staying SMART: Specific, Measurable, Attainable, Realistic and within a specific Timeframe with your goals. You will need to identify detailed steps for each one of the "Goals" you wrote in Step 2 above.

The following shows a sample of one life area (education) and one goal and its action steps. You will only start your plan here, but it must end up as complete as possible. It needs to become a part of the substance of your daily schedule, and thus, your life (so you can make your life happen). Remember, this is *not* written in stone—not your purpose, or any of the goals or steps. Just as in a strategic plan in business, things change. Life has a funny way of shifting from time to time, requiring adjustments in timing, steps, and resources. Sometimes you might simply change your mind, but to get anywhere, you must start somewhere.

For more detailed instructions, try a handout from this site: www.mpace.org/html/AnnualConference/arizona/Powerpoints/creatingastrategiclifeplanhandout.doc.

Good luck, and happy planning!

THIS AUTHOR'S SAMPLE OF A STRATEGIC LIFE PLAN

Life Area: Education
Goals: Finish my doctoral degree at Cambridge Theological Seminary, Byesville, Ohio
Action Steps
- Enroll and get accepted into the program
- While waiting apply for financial aid

Deadlines: By the end of winter term 2010

Directions: Use this format in developing your strategic life plan on a separate sheet of paper, or in your notebook, or journal:

My life area:
My goals:
My action steps:
My deadlines:

Remember, if you fail to plan, you plan to fail!

If you go to work on your goals, your goals will go to work on you. If you go to work on your plan, your plan will go to work on you. Whatever good things we build end up building us.

—Jim Rohn

A clear vision, backed by definite plans, gives you a tremendous feeling of confidence and personal power. . . . People with clear, written goals, accomplish far more in a shorter period of time than people without them could ever imagine.

—Brian Tracy

If you want to be happy, set a goal that commands your thoughts, liberates your energy, and inspires your hopes.

—Andrew Carnegie

Twenty years from now you will be more disappointed by the things that you didn't do than by the ones you did do. So throw off the bowlines. Sail away from the safe harbor. Catch the trade winds in your sails. Explore. Dream. Discover.

—Mark Twain

Priorities—A hundred years from now it will not matter what my bank account was, the sort of house I lived in, or the kind of car I drove, but the world may be different because I was important in the life of another person. Leave a legacy!

—Author unknown

When you sow an action, you reap a habit; when you sow a habit, you reap a character; and when you sow a character, you reap a destiny.

—Zig Ziglar

Go reap your destiny! What are you waiting for? Develop your personal strategic plan right now and leave a legacy!

This Day We Sailed On!
By Tim Adsit ©
Tuesday, December 29, 2009
Bend, Oregon

Columbus kept a journal as he sailed over the Atlantic Sea
While onboard the Pinta, the Nina, and the Santa Marie.
During his famous adventure to discover the New World,
On many nights, encouraged, as his continuing voyage unfurled,

He recorded the day's progress on his journal page,
Where, often he penned this simple and determined message.
This day we sailed on! This day we sailed on!
Christopher Columbus sailed on.

He was driven by the hope of discovery,
And the thrill of exploring uncharted territory.
Though few of us go searching for new worlds these days,
Our lives are nevertheless abundant with daily discoveries as we live, learn, and grow in new ways.

Just like in our business journey and adventure, our imaginations must be stimulated, curiosity sparked, the drive to discover rekindled.
Our journey must be fun, interesting, intriguing, and challenging beyond expectation,
But realizing it's the journey that counts, not the ultimate destination.

A ship is safe when it is in the harbor,
But this is not what ships are for.
The adventure, the challenge, and the rewards are for those who take the journey,
So, go ahead, begin your adventure, discover what's inside and your ability to be set free.

Like Columbus, never give up, but keep on keeping on,
And say at the end of the day, this day we sailed on!
Come along and soar with me, yearn to be free,
And do whatever it takes to fulfill your ultimate destiny and leave a legacy.

Directions: The author's personal strategic life plan goal examples continue here. You are strongly encouraged to write your goals down on a separate sheet of paper, or in your notebook or journal in each of the thirteen major life goal plan areas using the template and format found below for each goal area.

Goal: Spiritual

To continue helping to fulfill the Great Commission found in Matthew 28:19–20.

Objectives:
1. Witness to others when the occasion arises
2. Continue financially supporting God's missions work monthly
3. Continue writing religious and inspirational books and poems and get them published
4. Continue praying to discern whether God's will is for me to establish a new church, school, and seminary where I live, work for someone else in a Christian school, or some other capacity
5. Tithe 10 to 20 percent of earnings I make from all business ventures and books
6. Continue Bible study and daily faith periods of at least thirty minutes per day

Priority	Action (Tasks)	Due Date	Person Responsible	Results/Progress to Date/Contingencies

Goal: Family/Parenting

To daily be a loving and faithful husband to my wife and to be a loving, caring, and nurturing father and grandfather to my children and grandchildren, and help them grow and develop as responsible citizens for the twenty-first century.

Objectives:
1. Lead a more balanced life, putting family second only to God
2.
3.

Priority	Action (Tasks)	Due Date	Person Responsible	Results/Progress to Date/Contingencies

Goal: Friends/Social

To cultivate friendships with those I know in and around where I live by doing something positive socially with each other at least once per month such as dinner, movie, home visits for conversation, games, etc.

Objectives:
1.
2.
3.

Priority	Action (Tasks)	Due Date	Person Responsible	Results/Progress to Date/Contingencies

Goal: Community

During the next two months, market my presence to the community as a writer, consultant, independent business owner, and pastor via TV interviews, newspaper interviews, handbills to funeral homes, flower shops, jewelers, and city hall justice of the peace, cards on local card boards.

Objectives:
 1.
 2.
 3.

Priority	Action (Tasks)	Due Date	Person Responsible	Results/Progress to Date/Contingencies

Goal: Health

To be in the best shape physically, mentally, and emotionally I am capable of being or becoming from age sixty-three on.

Objectives:
 1. To lose 60 lbs per year for the next three years or 180 lbs total. (Started at 383.5 lbs - 180 lbs = 203.5 lbs weight goal)
 2. To continue taking all prescribed medicines regularly to control various diseases I have including bi-polar disorder, type two diabetes, gout, and high cholesterol.
 3. To walk or tone-up exercise at least five days per week, stay on Nutrisystem D diet or the equivalent and maintain ideal weight once reached.

Priority	Action (Tasks)	Due Date	Person Responsible	Results/Progress to Date/Contingencies

Goal: Educational/Intellectual

To continue to stimulate my mind and to grow intellectually daily for the rest of my life.

Objectives:
1. Continue reading at least thirty minutes per day from the Bible, some other positive thinking book, or pleasure reading book preferably just before bedtime or at other times available throughout the day.
2. Continue to listen to positive thinking tapes or to beautiful music.
3. Continue professional development in my current fields of current interest and/or expertise by reading, taking online classes, or attending seminars and workshops in the areas of teaching, educational administration, consulting, writing, poetry, marketing, publishing, ministry, or entrepreneurship.

Priority	Action (Tasks)	Due Date	Person Responsible	Results/Progress to Date/Contingencies

Goal: Career/Vocational/Professional/Entrepreneurial

Objectives:
1. Continue to apply to selected Oregon, Washington, Northern California, or Idaho public and/or private sector superintendent/principal positions.
2. Continue my consulting business and expand it with my personal strategic planning book by developing a website and driving more web traffic to the site.
3. Continue writing, marketing, publishing business (TLAW, Inc.) and update my website driving more traffic to the site.
4. Continue and expand my Internet franchising business with a goal of becoming at least platinum with a $2,500/month net income within eighteen months.
5. Start a real estate investing business, funds permitting.

Priority	Action (Tasks)	Due Date	Person Responsible	Results/Progress to Date/Contingencies

Goal: Recreational

Objectives:
1. Continue to hunt, fish, camp, hike, do photography, and write poetry outdoors for as long as I am able.
2. Continue to expand poetry, drawing and painting hobbies and take a class in each area at COCC.
3. During the next ten years, travel to Mexico, Brazil, China, Israel, Australia, New Zealand, and selected parts of Europe as a part of my research for books as funds permit such travel.
4. Continue playing golf and tennis as funds, health, and fitness level allow.

Priority	Action (Tasks)	Due Date	Person Responsible	Results/Progress to Date/Contingencies

Goal: Financial

To remain debt free except for house and car payments and monthly living expenses.

Objectives:
1. Own no credit cards and use only debit/credit cards that come from my checking account.
2. Pay cash for all small and medium purchases not part of regular monthly expenses (for example, a new digital camera, a tennis racket, tuition for an art class, etc.).
3. Establish savings funds or accounts for the following goals on my "bucket list": The down payment or outright purchase of a small thirteen- to twenty-two-foot new or used travel trailer; a small log cabin on a piece of ground I will purchase with all utilities already present and a slab for my RV; funds to travel to the places mentioned above under recreational goals; funds to pay the down payment or outright purchase of a new or used ATV; funds for real estate investing or other kinds of investments (stocks, bonds, etc.), funds to purchase a greater amount of life insurance and/or health insurance to help insure that if something should happen to me, my wife, children, and grandchildren will be more secure.

Priority	Action (Tasks)	Due Date	Person Responsible	Results/Progress to Date/Contingencies

Goal: Housing

To continue to maintain our primary Bend home and doing only those projects to gain equity such as a kitchen, bathroom, laundry room remodel or outside improvements such as adding a hot tub, a small storage building, improving landscaping in back and front yards, killing weeds, adding a view deck off the upstairs bedroom, and cleaning out the gutters.

Objectives:
 1.
 2.
 3.

Priority	Action (Tasks)	Due Date	Person Responsible	Results/Progress to Date/Contingencies

Goal: Transportation

To pay off existing vehicles and buy either new or one- or two-year-old used vehicles of our choice within six years' time.

Objectives:
 1.
 2.
 3.

Priority	Action (Tasks)	Due Date	Person Responsible	Results/Progress to Date/Contingencies

Chapter Seven

Personal Strategic Plan Summary

> Strategic planning is a process by which we can envision the future and develop the necessary procedures and operations to influence and achieve that future.
>
> —Clark Crouch

WHERE DO YOU GO FROM HERE?

Together, we've taken a long and, perhaps for some, arduous and challenging journey through the process of developing your personal strategic plan. At this point, you may have mixed feelings—which is quite normal for many people. You may have an overwhelming feeling of "system overload" as you have identified the number of goals and actions you could, and perhaps should, be taking. However, reality suggests that if you try to "accomplish it all" right away, you are setting yourself up for failure. Planning efforts are most successful when they are designed to be taken a step at a time and to virtually ensure success at each step along the way. Don't forget that this is your personal strategic plan, one that needs to be implemented over several years—not weeks or months.

Furthermore, as this author has stressed throughout this book, you need to adapt this process to your own style and circumstance, not adopt it because some author wrote a book making it sound compelling. A plan, whether in your personal life or in your business, career, or professional life, is only useful if it gets implemented. And that has to be done in a manner that is comfortable, challenging, and achievable for you and for whoever else is helping in the creation of the plan.

TRANSLATE YOUR PERSONAL STRATEGIC PLAN INTO ACTION

One way to get started is to make a quick assessment of where you are now in your personal strategic planning process and do some tentative projections as to when it will be appropriate and realistic to concentrate on some of the steps. The author has included Personal Strategic Planning Forms in chapter 6 to assist you with this part of the process. These forms help you identify the goal, objectives related to that particular goal, priority, action tasks, due date, person or persons responsible, results, progress to date, and/or contingencies.

Note: You are not expected to literally use these forms in the book in a workbook-type fashion; rather, permission is herein given by the author to reproduce copies of the forms for your personal use, being sure to give credit where credit is due, since they are copyrighted.

SETTING A REALISTIC SCHEDULE

Once you have identified the steps in the process you intend to follow, you will want to establish a schedule for when each of the steps is to be started and completed. If you wish, you can use the Personal Strategic Plan Form found in chapter 6 as a tool for identifying each of the steps and an appropriate schedule for each.

SHARING AND COMMUNICATING YOUR PLANS WITH OTHERS

As George L. Morrisey points out in his classic book entitled *Creating Your Future: Personal Strategic Planning for Professionals*,

> if others will be actively involved in the determination of your plans, you need to secure their commitment to that process well in advance of when their assistance will be required so they can give it the attention it deserves. Also, while part of their motivation will probably be a desire to help you with your planning, they will be able to support the effort more enthusiastically if they see some personal benefit in that participation. This can range from awareness of where you are going and determining the impact of that on their own efforts to creating complementary plans of their own that might be personally rewarding....
>
> ...There are probably other people who are important to your future who may not play an active role in the development of your plans but need to be kept informed. These could include members of your family, current or potential em-

ployers, current or potential associates or employees, current or potential clients or customers, your banker or potential investors, as well as selected friends and professional colleagues. Sharing your plans with them, either at completion or while they are evolving, can be a powerful way of enlisting their support when it is needed. A well-laid-out plan demonstrates your own commitment to your future and is more likely to get the kind of positive response from others that you want. (Morrisey, 1992, p. 161)

TRACKING AND REVIEWING YOUR PLAN AND PROGRESS

One of the values and advantages of having your personal strategic plan written down and kept in either a three-ring binder or notebook along with a planning calendar is that they provide a vehicle for ensuring that you follow through with your commitments. Personally, this author likes to use a Franklin Planner for this purpose, but there are many other good products on the market.

In the initial stages of your personal strategic planning effort, the author recommends setting firm dates, at least once every three months, when you will take time out to review what you have accomplished, with both the development and implementation of your plan, the assessment of how well you are doing, what modifications need to be made, and where you need to invest more time and effort in order to remain on track.

WHEN, HOW, AND WHY TO MODIFY YOUR PERSONAL STRATEGIC PLAN

While you will make modifications periodically as a part of your tracking process, you need to formally review your personal strategic plan from top to bottom at least once a year, or whenever there is a significant change in your situation. Professional and business opportunities are likely to change, sometimes without your being consciously aware of it. Your personal values and philosophy may need to be revisited as you become more sensitive to their effect on your career and your life. New strategic issues may appear, and those you have been working on may become less critical, suggesting a shift in your priorities. Planning is a dynamic, living process that needs to reflect changing circumstances; it is not a rigid, static process that locks you into a given course of action regardless of what is happening in your world.

By now you should understand there is no one "right" way to develop and implement your personal strategic plan. It clearly must be adapted to your own specific style, needs, situation, and circumstances. You have to evaluate where you are now, where you want to be, what steps in the process are going to help you get there, and what represents a realistically challenging schedule for making your personal strategic plan come alive. The active involvement and support of others who are important to your future is also essential. Your plan must be seen, by you and by others, as a dynamic, living document that will guide you in a positive direction on your journey while permitting you to adjust your path or even move in a different direction when it makes sense to do so.

POINTS TO REMEMBER

There are eight foundational strategic questions in your personal strategic planning process. Answering these questions will bring clarity to your quest for an ideal business, career, or personal strategic plan.

1. Values: What are the values, virtues, qualities, and traits most important to you in your business and career?
2. Vision: If your business and career were perfect five years from today, what would they look like?
3. Mission: Based on your values and vision, specifically how do you achieve your vision?
4. Purpose: Every truly successful entrepreneur has an overarching purpose to his or her business—a genuine desire to serve others through their business. What is the purpose of your business and career?
5. Goals: What specific goals must you achieve in order to fulfill your ideal future vision in your business and career?
6. Knowledge and Skills: In what areas will you have to excel in the future in order to achieve your goals and fulfill your vision?
7. Habits: What specific habits of thought and action will you need to become the person who is capable of achieving the goals that you have set for yourself?
8. Daily Activities: What specific activities will you have to engage in each day to assure that you become the person you want to become and achieve the goals you want to achieve?

The quality of your thinking determines the quality of your life. The better the questions you ask of yourself, the better answers you will elicit. As you improve the quality of your thinking, the quality of everything that you do improves at the same time. Since there is really no limit as to how much you can improve the quality of your thinking, there is no real limit as to how much you can improve your life.

The Law of Correspondence says that your outer world will always be a reflection of your inner world. To change anything in your outer world, you must begin by changing what is going on in your inner world. The greater clarity you have with regard to who you are, what you want, and what you have to do to get there, the faster you will progress (as adapted from Kagan, Ronnie, March 2, 2010).

This book is a passport to your success and a way to make your dreams come true while still paying attention to reality. You are encouraged to dream on, dream big dreams, and then to make them happen!

References

Where there is no vision, the people perish.

—Proverbs 29:18

"A program to think, plan, and act strategically at all personal levels." (Adapted from www.CMOE.com/strategic-thinking.htm).

Adsit, Tim L., D. D. (2011). *Achieving Success for Kids: A Plan for Returning to Core Values, Beliefs, and Principles.* Lanham, MD: Rowman & Littlefield Education.

Adsit, Tim L. and Murdock, George. (2010). *Cutting Costs and Generating Revenues in Education,* 2nd Edition. Published in partnership with the Association of School Business Officials International. Lanham, MD: Rowman & Littlefield Education.

Austin, William J., Ed.D. (2002). *Strategic Planning for Smart Leadership: Rethinking Your Organization's Collective Future through a Workbook-Based, Three-Level Model.* Stillwater, OK: New Forum Press, Inc.

Author Unknown. (July 1, 2008). "The Importance of a Personal Strategic Plan," http://penstalker.com/whatevermighty/personal-development/the-importance-of-a-personal....

Barry, Bryan W. (1986). *Strategic Planning Workbook for Nonprofit Organizations*, St. Paul: Amherst H. Wilder Foundation.

Basham, V., and Lunenburg, F. (1989). "Strategic Planning, Student Achievement and School District Financial and Demographic Factors." *Planning and Changing*, 20(3), 158–171.

Belasco, J.A., and Stead, J.L. (1999). *Soaring with the Phoenix: Renewing the Vision, Reviving the Spirit, and Re-Creating the Success of Your Company.* New York: Warner Books.

Below, Patrick J., Morrisey, George L. and Acomb, Betty L. (1990) *The Executive Guide to Strategic Planning.* San Francisco: Jossey-Bass.

Birnbaum, William S. (1990). *If Your Strategy Is So Terrific, How Come It Doesn't Work?* New York: American Management Association.

References

Blair, Gary Ryan. (2011). *Create a Personal Strategic Plan.* www.motivationalcentral.com/goal-settings-personal-strategic-plan.html

Bland, Glenn. (1972). *Success: The Glenn Bland Method.* Wheaton, IL: Living Books, Tyndale House Publishers, Inc.

Bolman, L .G. and Deal, T. E. (1997). *Reframing Organizations: Artistry, Choice, and Leadership.* San Francisco: Jossey-Bass Publishers.

Conley, D. (1992, April). "Strategic Planning in America's Schools: An Exploratory Study." Paper presented at the annual meeting of the American Educational Research Association, San Francisco.

Conley, D. (1993, April). "Strategic Planning in Practice: An Analysis of Purposes, Goals, and Procedures." Paper presented at the annual meeting of the American Educational Research Association, Atlanta.

Cook, W. (1988). *Strategic Planning for America's Schools.* Arlington, VA: American Association of School Administrators.

Cook, William H. (1974). *Success, Motivation, and the Scriptures.* Nashville, TN: Broadman Press.

Dahl, Bernhoff A., M.D. (2008). *Optimize Your Life! 2008 Workbook Edition.* TrionicsUSA.com.

Drucker, P.F. (1973). *The Practice of Management.* New York: Harper and Row.

Goodstein, Leonard, Nolan, Timothy and Pfeiffer, J. William. (1993). *Applied Strategic Planning: How to Develop a Plan Than Really Works.* New York: McGraw-Hill.

Gouillart, F. (1995, May-June). "The Day the Music Died." *Journal of Business Strategy,* 16(3), p. 14–20.

Guralnik, D. (Ed.). (1986). *Webster's New World Dictionary* (2nd ed). Cleveland, OH: Prentice Hall Press.

Hamel, Gary and Prahalad, C. K. (1994). *Competing for the Future.* Boston: Harvard Business School Press.

Helgesen, S. (1996). "Leading from the Grass Roots." In F. Hesselbien, M. Goldsmith, and R. Beckhard (eds.), *The Leader of the Future* (pp. 19–24). San Francisco: Jossey-Bass Publishers.

Judy, R., and D'Amico, C. (1997). *Workforce 2020: Work and Workers in the 21st Century.* Indianapolis, IN: Hudson Institute.

Jurinski, J. (1993). *Strategic Planning.* New York: American Management Association.

Kagan, Ronnie. (2010). "Personal Strategic Planning—8 Foundational Strategic Questions." www.ronniekagan.wordpress.com.

Kennedy, P. (1993). *Preparing for the Twenty-First Century.* New York: Vintage Books.

Kirk, Janis Foord. (2004). *Survivability: Career Strategies for the New World of Work.* Kirk Communications, Inc.

Knoke, W. (1996). *Bold New World: The Essential Road Map to the Twenty-First Century.* New York: Kodansha International.

Lawler, E. E. (1996). *From the Ground Up: Six Principles for Building the New Logic Corporation.* San Francisco: Jossey-Bass Publishers.

Lucas, J. (1997). *Fatal Illusions.* New York: American Management Association.

Mazur, Helene. (2007). "Personal Strategic Planning—Why Wait?" Princeton, NJ: Princeton Performance Dynamics. www.ppdbusinesscoaching.com/archive/personal.html

McCune, S. (1986). *Strategic Planning for Educators*. Alexandria, VA: Association for Supervision and Curriculum Development.

Miech, Edward J., (1995, Fall). "The Rise and Fall of Strategic Planning and Strategic Planning in Education." *The Harvard Education Review*. www.hepg.org/her/abstract/310

Mintzberg, H. (1994). *The Rise and Fall of Strategic Planning*. New York: The Free Press.

Morrisey, George L. (1992). *Creating Your Future: Personal Strategic Planning for Professionals*. San Francisco: Berrett-Koehler.

Norris, D. M. and Poulton, N. L. (1991). *A Guide for Planners*. Ann Arbor, MI: The Society for College and University Planning.

Petersen, John L. (2008). *A Vision for 2012: Planning for Extraordinary Change*. Golden, CO: Fulcrum Publishing, p. 3.

Pinchot, G. and Pinchot, E. (1994). *The End of Bureaucracy and the Rise of the Intelligent Organization*. San Francisco: Berrett-Koehler Publishers, Inc.

Rowley, D. J., Lujan, H. D., and Dolence, M. G. (1997). *Strategic Change in Colleges and Universities*. San Francisco: Jossey-Bass Publishers.

Schein, E. H. (1992). *Organizational Culture and Leadership*. San Francisco: Jossey-Bass.

Senge, P. (1996). *Leading Learning Organizations: The Bold, the Powerful, and the Invisible*. In F. Hesselbien, M. Goldsmith, and R. Beckhard (eds.), *The Leader of the Future* (pp. 41–58). San Francisco: Jossey-Bass Publishers.

Sloan, Richard. (May 12, 2011). "Personal Strategic Planning." Synergy Blog, Mastering Small Business. www.synergysharedsolutions.com/2011/05/12/personal-strategic-planning/ pp. 1–2.

Steiner, George A. (1979). *Strategic Planning: What Every Manager Must Know*. New York: Free Press.

Tracey, Brian. (2011). "Wealth without Guilt: Create Your Personal Strategic Plan." March 7, 2011. www.wealthwhisperer.Blogspot.com/2011/03/create-your-personal-strategic-plan-by-html.

Wall, S. J., and Wall, S. R. (1995, Autumn). "The Evolution (not the Death) of Strategy." *Organizational Dynamics* 24(2), p. 6.

Wheatley, M. J. (1996). *Leadership and the New Science: Learning About Organization from an Orderly Universe (Cassette Recording)*. San Bruno, CA: Audio Literature.

Wheelwright, Verne. Adapted from, www.personalfutures.net/ and www.yourpersonalfuture.blogspot.com/

www.CMOE.com/strategicthinking.htm

About the Author

Dr. Tim L. Adsit has excelled as a "change agent" throughout his career and served as a professional executive administrator in school districts that value visionary leadership and continuous improvement in student learning and achievement.

Adsit is uniquely qualified to write this book by a record of successful and progressively responsible service in the following positions: superintendent; director of curriculum, instruction, school improvement, assessment, personnel services, rural schools, interim special education, and grant writing; management consultant; elementary and secondary principal; high school, middle school, and elementary school teacher; private Christian school executive administrator/principal; college graduate teaching assistant; and adjunct summer visiting professor. This illustrates his ability to play a dynamic leadership role in the field of education.

He possesses a broad knowledge of all phases of educational administration, and brings diverse, demonstrated, successful experience in strategic planning ranging from public and private school districts as small as 60 students to as large as 12,500 students. He also has had experience serving as superintendent/principal in one of the largest public boarding schools in the nation. More recently, he has started a small businesses of his own.

Tim received his MEd and BS in education from Oregon State University, and did post-graduate work in educational administration at the University of Oregon. He also received his Doctor of Divinity in December of 2009 from Cambridge Theological Seminary. Tim resides in Prarie City, Oregon. Should you wish to contact the author, you may reach him at: timads@bendbroadband.comor call his office at 503-991-9446.

www.ingramcontent.com/pod-product-compliance
Lightning Source LLC
Chambersburg PA
CBHW020753230426
43665CB00009B/585